POLITICAL CORRECTNESS

Point/Counterpoint

Philosophers Debate Contemporary Issues
General Editors: James P. Sterba and Rosemarie Tong

This new series will provide a philosophical angle to debates currently raging in academic and larger circles. Each book will be a short volume (around 200 pages) in which two prominent philosophers debate different sides of an issue. *Political Correctness: For and Against,* by Marilyn Friedman and Jan Narveson, inaugurates the series. Other possible topics include the canon, the ethics of abortion rights, and the death penalty. For more information contact Professor Sterba, Department of Philosophy, University of Notre Dame, Notre Dame, IN 46566.

POLITICAL CORRECTNESS

For and Against

Marilyn Friedman and Jan Narveson

ROWMAN & LITTLEFIELD PUBLISHERS, INC.

ROWMAN & LITTLEFIELD PUBLISHERS, INC.

Published in the United States of America
by Rowman & Littlefield Publishers, Inc.
4720 Boston Way, Lanham, Maryland 20706

3 Henrietta Street
London WC2E 8LU, England

British Cataloging in Publication Information Available

Library of Congress Cataloging-in-Publication Data

Friedman, Marilyn
Political correctness : for and against / Marilyn Friedman and Jan
Narveson.
   p. cm.
Includes bibliographical references and index.
1. Political correctness.   2. Feminist theory.   I. Narveson, Jan
II. Title.
BD175.5.P65F75   1995   306'.0973—dc20   94-33880   CIP

ISBN 0-8476-7985-3 (cloth: alk. paper)
ISBN 0-8476-7986-1 (pbk: alk. paper)

Printed in the United States of America

 ^{TM} The paper used in this publication meets the minimum requirements of
American National Standard for Information Sciences—Permanence of
Paper for Printed Library Materials, ANSI Z39.48–1984.

Contents

Preface

Our topic is "political correctness," a diverse array of the most controversial academic and cultural issues of our day. New fields of study, such as women's studies and African American studies, new disciplinary approaches, such as multiculturalism and feminism, new campus practices, such as speech codes, and new cultural critiques, such as those of truth and of politics-free intellectual inquiry—all these and more have become the terrains of bitter intellectual warfare in contemporary Western societies. In the estimations of some, the survival of those cultures depends on the outcome of the struggle. Our collaboration in this debate is premised on the possibility and the urgency of a negotiated settlement as well as the conviction that genuine dialogue—honest, open, engaged, and mutually respectful—is still too rare a phenomenon when it comes to political correctness.

The materials on which we base our essays include scholarly and popular works that debate political correctness in Canada and the United States. The debate has clearly entered mass media, and rightly so. Accordingly, we have written a volume that is, we think, accessible to a wide audience, not just philosophers and not just students or teachers or researchers. Our intended audience is the generally educated public, anyone who cares about the state of the academy today and who is concerned about the role and importance of education in culture at large.

The scope of our discussion ranges across an assortment of topics chosen by each of us because of our respective interests. We do not offer a comprehensive survey of all possible issues of political correctness. We discuss campus speech codes, the Western canon, multiculturalism, truth and objectivity, affirmative action, and feminism.

Our approach is one of friendly debate and nonrancorous dialogue. We seek careful consideration of the issues. After writing our lead essays separately and engaging in a fierce round of dueling e-mails over the shared results, we came closer to mutual comprehension, even if not

to agreement. Our responses, we hope, reflect that enriched understanding.

We owe thanks to Jim Sterba, our series editor, and Jon Sisk, editor-
in-chief, at Rowman & Littlefield for providing us with the welcome
opportunity to forge this exchange. We also thank Rowman & Littlefield's assistant editor, Jennifer Ruark, for her accommodating steward-
ship of the project at later stages.

Codes, Canons, Correctness, and Feminism

Marilyn Friedman

In the fall of 1990, "political correctness" in the academy emerged as a national news media preoccupation. Political correctness (PC) comprises a host of academic reforms and attitudes that, according to their critics, are destroying higher education and threatening national survival.

The alleged culprit is the academic left, a group encompassing feminists, multiculturalists, Marxists, and deconstructionists. In their teaching and scholarship, these leftist academics are supposed to have launched a full-scale attack on Western civilization. They have replaced the classical works of Western culture with third world, anti-Western trash and have forsaken standards of truth, objectivity, and merit of any sort. They have consolidated their academic power by smuggling unqualified women and minorities into positions of educational dominance and by ruthlessly quashing dissenting voices. Their multicultural machinations will soon surely fragment the United States into an intellectual Yugoslavia.[1]

From the standpoint of the left, however, the picture is quite different. The reforms in question are intended to revamp a host of traditional academic practices and attitudes that constitute the *real* malaise of higher education. The real correctness to worry about, from a leftist perspective, is the "rectitude" of those traditionalists who resist the growing cultural diversity of academia today. The policies of the critics of political correctness would return us to the deplorably homogeneous and exclusionary educational world of yesterday.

The left has, accordingly, raised critical questions about the quality of everything academic, from esoteric scholarly research to the interper-

1

sonal dynamics of daily campus life. Most importantly, the left has challenged European, American, heterosexual, and masculine biases that continue to permeate traditional research and pedagogy. This challenge has rejuvenated age-old skeptical inquiries into such venerated notions as truth, objectivity, impartiality, and disinterested criticism. In addition, new fields of study have emerged to promote research into, and by, hitherto misrepresented or unrepresented peoples, fields such as African American studies and women's studies. Furthermore, the preeminence of Western canonical literatures in the humanities and social sciences has diminished as traditional disciplines themselves have witnessed the growth of new research paradigms emphasizing race, gender, ethnicity, and sexual orientation as analytical categories.

The left has also turned its attention to the campus environment. For some time now, the left has been contesting the persistently low numbers of women and certain minority groups in specific academic populations—students, faculty, or administration, as appropriate. The results of these challenges include the notorious affirmative action plans. The left has also worried about campus climates that are often inhospitable to students who are not white, not male, and not heterosexual. These concerns have led to student behavior codes that penalize insulting epithets used against women and minorities.

All of these developments fit under an umbrella rubric: the promotion of diversity and multiculturalism in academic life. Calls for diversity and multiculturalism have become anathema to many traditionalists and other opponents of these innovations. Most of what is connected to the pursuit of multiculturalism is now ridiculed as being "politically correct." This label was co-opted from an earlier self-critical but friendly use by leftists themselves meant to deflate their own excesses with humor and irony. When the charge is deployed by critics of multiculturalism, however, the humor and irony vanish.

Although multiculturalism has had its share of defenders, there is still much that remains to be said on behalf of these controversial and challenging academic developments. In this spirit, my discussion deals with four topics that fit under the general heading of political correctness: campus speech codes, the Western literary canon, the concept of truth, and feminism.

Speech Codes

A number of academic institutions have recently tried to implement a novel sort of student behavior code. The codes in question penalize students who use racist, sexist, or homophobic "hate speech" to insult other students. Schools that have experimented with these codes include Stanford University, the University of Michigan, and the University of Wisconsin. The codes have been drafted in an attempt to protect from verbal harassment certain groups of students who are otherwise vulnerable to taunts and insults. The intent of the codes is thus salutary. Nevertheless, they have been widely challenged as unjustified infringements on the First Amendment guarantee of freedom of speech.

Some of the challenges have taken legal form and speech codes are not faring well in the courts. In the fall of 1991, for example, the University of Wisconsin code was overturned by a U.S. district court that held that the code violated the constitutional guarantee of freedom of expression.[2] In 1992, the Supreme Court overturned a St. Paul, Minnesota, ordinance that similarly attempted to regulate racial and sexual epithets.[3]

Defenders of speech codes have tried to argue that the insults in question do not merit First Amendment protection because they are a variety of what the Supreme Court has called "fighting words." As defined by the Court in 1942, fighting words are those insults "which by their very utterance inflict injury or tend to incite an immediate breach of the peace."[4] In recent years, this court doctrine has been greatly modified but not entirely eliminated. Fighting words can still be penalized provided they pose the "clear and present danger" of a breach of the peace, for instance, a violent reaction by the insulted party.[5]

Unfortunately for the codes, court doctrine requires that an imminent danger be demonstrated in each and every case; no particular type of language can be declared punishable in advance. Nevertheless, in its 1992 decision regarding the St. Paul, Minnesota, ordinance, the Supreme Court allowed that fighting words could be banned provided the ban was not restricted to certain categories of insults, such as those focusing only on sex or race.[6] Thus, academic speech codes, if carefully drafted, may yet survive their court challenges.

The codes have, nevertheless, faced strong opposition. Regrettably, code critics too often seem far more bothered by requirements *not to express* racism, sexism, and homophobia in public than they are by the prevalence of those attitudes. In this context, however, I will not be defending academic speech codes as such. My concern focuses instead on some disturbing features in the campaign that has been waged against the codes by some of their critics.

First of all, code critics suggest that speech codes are being used to suppress criticism of policies such as affirmative action and abortion rights by treating such criticism as if it were racist or sexist language.[7] To my knowledge, this suggestion is incorrect. Speech codes have been neither designed nor implemented to suppress genuine debate over controversial issues. During the University of Wisconsin's brief period of speech code enforcement, students were penalized for calling other students such obscenities as "fucking bitch" and "fat-ass nigger."[8] If speech codes were used to punish criticism of, say, abortion or affirmative action, then that would be misuse of the codes. Misuse, however, does not show that codes against racist or sexist insults are themselves wrong. The real issue is whether or not it is legally and morally appropriate for an academic institution to penalize genuine group-based insults used by some students against other students.[9]

A second problem with the campaign being waged against speech codes is its occasional hypocrisy.[10] Code critics insistently invoke the constitutional and moral halo of a right to freedom of expression, or free speech. There have been a variety of threats to free speech in recent years, however, and someone who really wants to protect that right should have challenged all of them. Code critics have not always been so consistent.

A genuine defender of free speech would have objected to George Bush's executive order that prohibited employees in federally funded health clinics from counseling their patients about abortion services.[11] That is, a genuine defender of free speech would have been just as concerned then about the abortion "gag rule" as she was about campus speech codes. The morality of abortion was not at issue; the question was one of free speech, in this case, the freedom of a health care worker to tell a client about a legally available medical service.

Now, someone might try to justify an abortion "gag rule" by arguing that it is all right to curb the speech of anyone who is even partly supported by tax dollars if the taxpayers object to what is being said. Anti-abortion taxpayers do not want their tax dollars used to support even the merest mention of abortion. Remember, however, that opinion polls show repeatedly that only a minority of U.S. taxpayers are flatly opposed to abortion under any circumstances.[12] The relevant principle would have to be something like this: speech that is otherwise legal may be suppressed when it is partly supported by tax money and conflicts with the values of some taxpayers.

That principle, however, condones campus speech codes just as readily as it condones the abortion gag rule. Some taxpayers, I, for one, do not want our tax dollars going to support public universities in which some students may with impugnity call other students "niggers," "bitches," and "faggots." Thus, using the gag rule as a model, college administrators at publicly funded universities are entitled to implement codes that penalize hate speech, as long as at least some of the taxpayers in that state oppose it. The same argument would hold by analogy for private universities whose financial supporters oppose hate speech on their campuses.

On the other hand, if it is wrong for universities to stifle racial and sexual insults, even when their financial supporters oppose such speech, then gag rules are also wrong that prevent health care workers from using polite speech to describe legally available medical services. Consistency calls for the opponents of speech codes to condemn abortion gag rules in the same breath in which they condemn the codes. In the case of those who have not done so, it is legitimate to wonder whether they are really defending all free speech or merely speech of a certain sort, in this case, racist, sexist, or homophobic insults.[13]

The third problem with the opposition to speech codes is that it sometimes blurs the issues and switches to a different target. Speech code critics sometimes try to make it seem as if leftist advocacy by itself is as much a violation of free speech rights as are the formal codes. Criticizing speech codes thereby becomes a vehicle for covertly denouncing leftist expression as such without having to respond to its content.

Nat Hentoff, for example, a journalist and veteran free speech proponent, complains that students who advocate leftist views in the classroom create a "chilling atmosphere" that leads other students to censor themselves. According to Hentoff, on one occasion at New York University Law School, a "sizable number" of leftist law students challenged the use of a case that was assigned for moot court competition. The case involved a divorced father who was trying to gain custody of his children because their mother, his ex-wife, had become a lesbian. The students who objected to using the case in moot court apparently thought that lesbian and gay students in the class might be offended by someone arguing on behalf of the father. A chilling atmosphere resulted, according to Hentoff, in which those students who wanted to discuss the case "censored themselves" from saying so.[14]

Why, we should ask, is Hentoff upset about this? Those leftist students who challenged the case were merely exercising their rights to free speech. Based on Hentoff's own principles, the fact that some students were chilled by the expression of this view is irrelevant. In a context of virtually unrestricted freedom in the expression of ideas, some people will sometimes say what others find to be chilling. Unrestricted freedom of speech is not a protection merely for those who want to insult women, minorities, lesbians, and gays.

Hentoff opposes speech codes because he does not think that black, female, lesbian, or gay students should be ''insulated from barbed language.'' They should have to learn to respond to language they do not like ''with more and better language of their own.'' On this subject, Hentoff quotes approvingly the words of Gwen Thomas, a ''black community college administrator from Colorado.'' Thomas opposes speech codes on the grounds that students should have to learn ''how to deal with adversarial situations.''[15]

Evidently, Hentoff thinks that non-leftist students should *not* have to learn how to deal with adversarial situations. They should not have to learn to respond, with more and better language of their own, to the leftist views that chill the atmosphere for them.

The problem of free speech is that when a view is expressed by a majority of those present, or even a vocal minority, it might well suppress those who think differently. Rather than being part of the speech code framework, however, this group pressure is precisely the result of having no prohibitions on the relevant speech. Facing virtually no restrictions, majority opinion or outspoken minority opinion will range wherever it can, and exert the pressures that it exerts. Sometimes the most vocal opinions will be leftist, and when this happens, conservatives and other nonleftists are the ones who will feel a bit of a chill.

If Hentoff really cares about freedom of *all* speech, he should gallantly accept the chilling effects exerted by vocal leftists no less than the chilling effects exerted by conservatives, racists, and bigots of all sorts as the price to be paid for whatever value we gain from freedom of speech. Why should blacks, women, and certain others have to devote extra time to responding to chilling or adversarial speech against them if students who dissent from leftist views are permitted to enjoy the luxury of not having to respond to their adversaries? After all, leftist students are entitled to exercise their own vaunted free speech rights, too.

I do not promote speech codes. I do support values of mutual respect, civility, and courtesy wherever possible—and most of the time, university life is a place where these values are eminently possible. Ideally, the members of our academic citizenries (and of our societies at large) should regard hate speech as so morally intolerable that they object to it vocally and point out the bigoted attitudes manifested by such speech. My recommendation, then, is to avoid the use of formal speech codes but to make sure that the issue of offensive speech does not die with the codes.

The Western Canon

Another area of contention between cultural leftists and their critics has to do with the Western canon, that loose assortment of literary works commonly regarded as the best of the Western tradition. In the view of Roger Kimball, author of *Tenured Radicals*, all so-called academic radicals "exhibit a pervasive animus against the achievements and values of Western culture; all systematically subjugate the teaching and study of literature to political imperatives." From Kimball's standpoint, the radical takeover of the Modern Language Association is one vivid sign of nasty goings-on that have "infected" the entire "academic study of the humanities in this country."[16]

Kimball's attack on these anticanonical attitudes and approaches generally falls into two major areas of concern, both of which typify the views about the Western canon presented by most critics of political correctness. Kimball argues, for one thing, that the canonical literature of the West is of "universal human interest." The canon speaks to people "*across* the barriers of time, geography, social system, religious belief, to say nothing of the currently favored barriers of sex, class, race, and ethnic origin." Kimball believes that a multiculturalist approach leads to an "obsession with one's race, one's sex, one's sexual preferences, one's ethnic origin." One thereby gains a "political cause" and loses "the freedom of disinterested appreciation" of universal values. I refer to this defense of the canon as the "universality of the Western canon" view.[17]

The second area of Kimball's concern is that criticism and disregard of the Western canon are, in some fundamental way, threatening to our society. For Kimball, the heart of the "multiculturalist ethos" is the view that "all cultures are equally valuable" and that a preference for Western culture is, therefore, "ethnocentric and racist." The academic developments embodying this view, in Kimball's opinion, involve "the destruction of the fundamental premises that underlie . . . our . . . liberal democratic polity." To reject the Western canon's primacy is, therefore, to reject the "quintessentially Western ideas [that] are bedrocks of our political . . . system."[18]

What are some of these allegedly bedrock ideas? They include commitments to rationality, individual rights, the "ideals of disinterested criticism, color-blind justice, and advancement according to merit, not according to sex, race, or ethnic origin."[19] The reverent study of these ideas is necessary to preserve our "liberal democratic polity."

This view is not unique to Kimball; among opponents of political correctness, it is widespread. Prior to his appointment as "drug czar" under the Reagan administration, William Bennett had been the humanities czar; in the early 1980s, he directed the National Endowment for the Humanities. In that capacity, Bennett published a pamphlet entitled *To Reclaim a Legacy: A Report on the Humanities in Higher Education.*[20] Bennett's pamphlet calls for a renewed curricular emphasis on the "great epochs" of Western civilization, which provided the "glue that binds together our pluralistic nation." That glue consists of the founding principles of "justice, liberty, government with the consent of the governed, and equality under law." Universities in the United States need to teach these materials in order to convey the "accumulated wisdom of our civilization," and, we may infer, to prevent the nation from coming unglued.[21]

Other defenders of the Western canon foretell the impending disaster in still more alarming terms. Donald Kagan, until recently the dean of Yale College, has written that our "democratic, liberal society" will be *imperiled* if Western civilization and culture are not placed at the center of our studies.[22] Allan Bloom evidently thought the battle had already been lost. In the thesis synopsis of his best-selling indictment of academe, *The Closing of the American Mind*, Bloom declares that higher education has both "impoverished the souls of today's students" and "failed democracy."[23] I refer to this second defense of the Western canon as the "well-being of our society" view.

To summarize, critics of the left commonly raise two main concerns about the declining study of the Western canon. First, the canon contains works of universal human interest, which speak to everyone; this is the universality of the canon view. Second, the canon contains works that articulate the foundational principles of our liberal democracy, principles that we criticize and disregard at peril of our nation; this is the wellbeing of our society view.[24]

My contention is that neither defense of the Western canon supports the opposition to multiculturalism. The Western canon can be enlisted to show this. Each defense suffers from at least three problems.

Consider first the universality of the Western canon view. Critics of political correctness present us with what purports to be an unbiased claim in defense of the ability of the Western canon to speak to people everywhere. This is a rather large group, including all those people around the world who have not received a Western-style education as well as those who have received no formal education at all. Rather than accept on faith the claim that the Western canon speaks to all these people, we need to ask for evidence. Is the claim about the universality of the Western canon based primarily on the judgments and evaluations of westerners themselves? If so, the potential for arrogance and ignorance looms large.

One familiar and canonical Western view of human nature has it that people are basically self-interested and inclined to be biased in their own favor. This view is a crucial underpinning for Thomas Hobbes's social contract theory and it plays a fundamental role in both John Locke's and John Stuart Mill's theories of representative government. A citizen who has no opportunity to express her own beliefs on matters of government at any level of political organization has no guarantee that her viewpoint is genuinely represented. Other persons, self-interested each, cannot ultimately be trusted to speak for her. It follows from this canonical Western view of human nature that any claims about the universality of Western cultural works that are made only or primarily by members of Western cultures are equally likely to be self-serving. The only reliable assertions of the Western canon's universally human interest would be those which substantially represented the diversity of individual perspectives around the globe.

In Kimball's view, the result of rejecting the preeminence of the Western canon is a "thoughtless egalitarianism" in which "all cultures are equally valuable."[25] On the contrary, questioning the universality of the Western canon need neither generate nor presume the substantive judgment that "all cultures are equally valuable." It need merely manifest a deep caution about the justifiability of cultural comparisons and grand sweeping generalizations. In addition, one may question the alleged universality of the Western canon without entirely abandoning it, as can be seen from my own reliance on certain canonical ideas. Thus, at least one very canonical Western conception of human nature (that it is self-interested) casts doubt on the credibility of any Westerner's assertions of the canon's universality.

The strongest evidence for thinking that the Western canon addresses genuinely universal interests would be that representatives of the great diversity of cultural perspectives around the world agreed to this claim in an ongoing dialogue. The relevant voices should speak for all viewpoints: female as well as male, poor as well as rich, black as well as white (and brown and beige). The project of representing those voices is exemplified by a curriculum that includes both non-Western works and noncanonical works of Western subcultures that are omitted from the Western canon. The strongest evidence for the universality of the Western canon can arise only out of this sort of lengthy and sustained intracultural and cross-cultural dialogue.

In emulation of one grand Western idea, I propose the following principle for assessing the interests addressed by cultural works: "No universalization without representation!" This approach is precisely what is embodied in multicultural curricula.

A second problem with the universality defense of the canon is that even if it is legitimate to proclaim certain interests as universal, the notion of addressing such interests is vague and uninformative. Any novel, however trashy, in which someone dies thereby touches on the universal human concern with death. Thus, merely addressing universal human interests is not enough to establish the preeminence of those works that are included in the Western canon.

Suppose that a defender of the canon were to argue that the Western canon does not merely address universal interests, but in addition promotes universal values and principles, ideals that apply to all human beings anywhere and anytime. This argument, however, would face problems of its own. The possible hubris involved in declaring that certain values apply to all human beings is only the most obvious one. There is also the difficulty of articulating those ideals in substantively specific and meaningful terms and then defending their alleged universality in just those terms—exactly the sort of problem that perennially challenges philosophers.

For example, it is easy to proclaim the universality of such abstractions as the good, the true, and the beautiful, or justice, liberty, and equality, but notoriously difficult to convince all, or even most, philosophers to accept any one specific account of those values. The traditional canon itself encourages critical reflection on any doctrine or method represented within the canon—including the very reliance on critical reflection.[26] Thus, again, one strand of thought in the canon undermines the ready presumption that any *well-specified* Western value-conceptions as such are universal.

Third, even if the canon does address universal human interests in substantively important ways, that does not by itself mean that we should study the Western canon to the exclusion of other literatures. To justify such exclusiveness, one could try to argue that the Western canon is, in some universal sense, qualitatively better than other canons and, therefore, more worth studying than any other. This would be a difficult claim to substantiate. The global superiority of the Western canon is easy enough to declare, but notoriously difficult to establish as impartial and uncontroversial truth.

Before we make cross-cultural comparisons of literary (or other cultural forms of) merit, we need to be sure that we are using criteria with cross-cultural legitimacy. The availability of such standards is a matter of serious dispute. Yet without them, we cannot be sure that the Western canon is more worth studying even by U.S. citizens than any other literary tradition that focuses on purportedly universal interests, values, or principles.

A critic of multiculturalism might respond at this point by arguing that we, in the United States, should study universally interesting ideas as presented in the Western canon in particular because our liberal democratic society is importantly a product of the Western tradition. Our culture, therefore, benefits if its citizenry is knowledgeable about the highest values and principles expressed in its own intellectual heritage.[27]

This response is certainly relevant. Notice, however, that this response shifts from the first to the second defense of the Western canon that I outlined earlier. Instead of continuing to insist on the canon's universality, this response asserts more locally that the well-being of our own society depends on its citizens being schooled in Western canonical works.

This second defense, unfortunately, is also questionable. For one thing, it is not always clear just what is at stake in these appeals to the well-being of our society. Is it the survival of the United States, or merely its flourishing? And, if the latter, just what sort of flourishing is in question? Moral integrity? Intellectual achievement? Spiritual revival? Or is it global economic competitiveness? Military dominance? And is it enough to flourish, to do well—or must we be tops? Globally supreme? *Numero uno*?

Does the achievement of these ends truly require that the Western canon be taught uncritically and exclusively? Will the United States honestly languish if some of our literature studies focus on race, sex, and ethnicity as analytical categories? If U.S. college students were to immerse themselves in *Moby Dick* and skip *The Color Purple*, would the Japanese really start to buy more Chevrolets?

There are no easy answers to the question of how to adjust various curricular elements in order to promote a citizenry that sustains this nation. The absence of easy answers is due partly to the fact that there are substantial disagreements over what it is about us that is indeed worth promoting. At this time, I offer only this observation. Our nation is not in imminent danger of collapse. Because our survival is not now threatened, we enjoy a marvelous luxury. We can afford to aim not merely for material sustenance and flourishing in the world, but also for moral sustenance and flourishing.

The Western canon, unfortunately, has major moral omissions. There are moral values and interests that it does not address in a substantial or sustained manner, however universal might be the range of interests that it does address. The Western canon in philosophy offers very little insight about how to negotiate the complicated ethnic pluralism that is a crucial and definitive feature of contemporary U.S. life. It also offers virtually no *critical* reflection on those traditional mainstays of human identity: femininity, masculinity, and the whole spectrum of gender-based social practices. The remedy for these omissions is to include multicultural studies in our curricula.

My recommendation is a curriculum that combines the Western canon with multicultural literatures. Roger Kimball, however, disparages such integrative approaches as "either an empty rhetorical gesture or a contradiction in terms."[28] Kimball, however, is wrong. His remark reduces the debate to a false dilemma by suggesting that even the whisper of multiculturalism means death to the canon. This is nonsense, designed, I fear, to scare us into suppressing the whole multicultural project. What is most ironic is that, in suppressing the non-Western and subcultural literatures that challenge Western ideas, Kimball is promoting just the sort of uncritical study of the Western canon that would kill its most valuable component: the spirit of open and critical inquiry.

There is one final irony about the belief that we must study the canon in order to secure the well-being of our society. This belief contradicts the claims of Western canon defenders that they want to return to an apolitical curriculum and that it is multiculturalism that politicizes the humanities. If the reason for studying the Western canon is that the survival or flourishing of our nation depends on it, then this agenda is *blatantly* political. In Kimball's view, our survival as a "liberal democratic polity" is at stake in these debates over the canon. What could be more political than an appeal to national interest?

It appears that the defenders of the Western canon are just as political as the critics of the canon, but with a different focus of concern. The canon promoters focus on the politics of nationhood, while the canon critics focus on the politics of sex, class, and ethnicity. Both camps, however, have deeply political commitments.[29] In this regard, the cultural leftists are vindicated, for this is exactly what we have been saying for quite some time.

I have examined two defenses of the Western canon, one that appeals to its supposed universality of interest, and one that appeals to its foundational role in sustaining our own society. My conclusion is that neither defense implies that multicultural literatures should not also have a prominent place in the academic curriculum.

Does this mean that I think we should scrap the obligatory study of the Western canon altogether and require students to study only non-Western and noncanonical Western works? No, it does not. Regardless of the worth of the Western canon, there is nevertheless good reason to require students in the United States to gain familiarity with at least some of it. The Western canon articulates the values that rationalize U.S. government and that predominate in U.S. culture. The influence of those institutions is virtually inescapable for anyone who lives in the United States. Education in the United States should certainly acquaint its students with the government and culture that dominate U.S. life.

My argument that students be required to study some of the Western canon does not assume (falsely) that the works of, say, the European Enlightenment constitute "our" cultural heritage. As a first-generation U.S. citizen, a Canadian resident for ten years, and the biological child of two Jewish immigrants from Eastern Europe, I am painfully aware of how heritages can be imposed, denied, misspent, and otherwise usurped. What is called "our" intellectual heritage simply consists of works that, in various ways, have established themselves as historically dominant in U.S. society. Those works influence my life regardless of whether or not I count them as mine.

Those who defend the Western canon on the grounds that the survival of our liberal democracy depends on it may think, rather naively, that students who learn about the political principles in the canon will automatically become "good citizens," compliant law-abiders who never question the nature, value, or policies of our public institutions. History, however, reveals that the contrary is often true. Major social movements in the United States have been sparked by the disillusioned recognition that some population group or other had been historically denied its share of the benefits of U.S. political ideals and values.[30]

Let us also remember that the Western canon is not a monolithic intellectual rationalization for the modern "heteropatriarchal-capitalist state." The canon provides at least some resources for foundational criticism of some predominant U.S. political ideals and values. Karl Marx, for example, is an established figure in the Western canon by the reckoning of most political and cultural theorists, both those who revere Marx as well as those who revile him.

Thus, I do not fear that a solid grounding in the Western canon or in U.S. political values will produce a compliant or acquiescent citizenry. Indeed, social criticism and political activism can become more knowledgeable and effective if informed by familiarity with the dominant traditions and institutions that are to be contested. Even the most extreme anti-Western political activist can grasp how prudent it is to "know thine enemy."

There are, however, no good reasons to confine U.S. students to the study of only the Western canon and very good reasons to promote in them a wider global orientation than is captured by the literary canon of the West. It is noteworthy that some defenders of the Western canon accept this point. They acknowledge the importance for U.S. citizens of having some familiarity with the many other increasingly interrelated cultures of our planet. Not all canon defenders share Kimball's rejection of an integrated approach.

When Western canon defenders make this concession, however, what they usually call for is the study of non-Western *classics*: the Koran, the *Analects* of Confucius, the Bhagavad Gita, and so on.[31] They continue to challenge many of the nonclassical and contemporary works used by multiculturalists to teach about non-Western cultures. I refer to this classics orientation as the "shallow global diversity" approach, since it incorporates only one strand of the cluster of concerns that animate the multiculturalist's vision. The shallow global diversity approach seizes hold of the concept of diversity per se and concedes that it is important for U.S. education to provide its students with some instruction about societies outside the United States and Europe. This concession is hardly a substantial one, however; anything less than this ought to be considered a national academic disgrace.

The shallow global diversity approach falls short of full-fledged, or *deep*, multiculturalism in at least two important respects. First, it pays inadequate attention to marginalized groups within Western societies, groups, such as women and nonwhites, that have historically been largely or entirely absent from the Western canon. Second, regarding cultures outside the West, the shallow global diversity approach continues to promote an uncritical canon worship. That is, it perpetuates the questionable assumption that the works that rise to "classic" status within a culture are therefore the best and most revealing works about that culture.

This assumption ignores entirely the social processes by which only some people in a society are enabled to rise to cultural prominence through the expression of ideas. Historically around the world, and still today in many parts of it, for example, women, much more often than men, are denied basic literacy—not to mention access to the higher reaches of formal education. These practices are thus not universally accessible, not reliably impartial, and therefore do not necessarily yield culturally representative literary classics. Questioning the process of canon formation, whether in our own culture or any other, is central to the multiculturalist's educational goals. Such questioning is absent from a shallow global diversity approach.

By ignoring this issue, the shallow global diversity approach attempts to shift the terms of the debate. Instead of denying the value of including non-Western cultures at all in the academic curriculum, shallow global diversity reformulates the controversy around the question of which particular non-Western works to include.

Shallow global diversity advocates criticize multiculturalists for using the *wrong* non-Western works. Dinesh D'Souza, for example, chides multiculturalists for their extensive use of *I, Rigoberta Menchu: An Indian Woman in Guatemala* in multicultural courses around the country.[32] Rigoberta Menchu is an illiterate Guatemalan of indigenous ancestry who told the story of her life to a French feminist named Elisabeth Burgos-Debray. Burgos-Debray, in turn, edited this book, based on Menchu's autobiographical oral narrative. D'Souza charges that Menchu is not representative of Guatemalan culture but was chosen for multiculturalist attention because she is what multiculturalists can regard as the "consummate victim," "pierced by the arrows" of racism, sexism, and colonialism. D'Souza regards Menchu as little more than a "mouthpiece for a sophisticated left-wing critique of Western society."[33]

D'Souza does not say *why* a victim of multiple oppressions is not a good representative of Guatemalan culture, but never mind that point. Never mind, also, that throughout his discussion, D'Souza refers to Menchu by her first name only. (D'Souza's male targets receive no such condescension.) D'Souza's discussion is most interesting because he staked his critique of multiculturalism on the gamble that Rigoberta Menchu was culturally trivial and that this example would serve to reveal the shallowness and hypocrisy of multiculturalist educational reforms. Happily, D'Souza lost his bet. Menchu has gained international recognition for her work as a leading peace activist on behalf of indigenous peoples throughout the Americas. D'Souza's argument appears in his best-seller, *Illiberal Education*, first published in 1991. Rigoberta Menchu was awarded the Nobel Peace Prize for 1992.[34]

In this instance, multiculturalists had a stroke of good luck. By contrast, most works that they would include in multicultural courses have not won the recognition of the Nobel peace committee and so they remain controversial.[35] It is, of course, legitimate to wonder just which works to use when teaching non-Western and noncanonical Western materials. How should this problem be decided? It seems appropriate to say, in regretably discredited terms, "let a hundred flowers blossom." If there are to be required courses in both Western and non-Western civilizations, then I urge that the readings mix canonical with noncanonical works in both areas.

There is no reason not to let the principle of faculty autonomy determine the exact selection of course materials in multicultural studies, just as it does throughout the rest of the curriculum. Throughout the curriculum, different teachers use different materials for the same courses, to suit their own research interests and pedagogical convictions. Why should this now change? One of my colleagues, for example, includes Hobbes's *Leviathan* in his history of ethics course; I usually do not. Even inside the small and highly exclusive Western philosophical canon, there is room for diversity. There is vastly greater variety outside the Western canon.

What about the matter of proportion? If students are required to study both Western and non-Western literary works, canonical as well as non-canonical in either domain, what should the distributions be? Shall we legislate a Western/non-Western fifty/fifty split? How about sixty/forty?

In general, there is no principled way to answer exactly the question of proportion. It is difficult to say just how much of the Western canon U.S. students need to study in order to be good, *critically reflective* citizens of their liberal democracy. Remember, current day "tenured radicals" belong to a generation that was reared on the traditional diet of required courses in "Western civ." Far from sustaining the common culture so desired by many defenders of the Western canon, the baby boom generation split early and decisively over major, nationwide political issues. In addition, the current young adult college generation, with fewer requirements in Western civ and considerably more access to African American studies, women's studies, and the rest, does not seem to be destroying the nation any more rapidly than their classically trained but radical elders. Again, I would leave the question of proportion to be decided by local academic constituencies and individual faculty autonomy.

Correctness

Before the word "correct" was drafted into service as an armament in the culture wars, it was a common household expression meaning, among other things, "true." The concept of truth, however, has also become a major arena of cultural struggle.

In September of 1992, the National Endowment for the Humanities published a pamphlet entitled *Telling the Truth: A Report on the State of the Humanities in Higher Education*, under the by-line of then-chair of the NEH, Lynne Cheney.[36] Lynne Cheney's husband, Dick Cheney, it may be recalled, served as secretary of defense in George Bush's administration. Conservative commentator George Will once observed that while Dick Cheney was defending the United States against foreign adversaries, Lynne Cheney was defending the country against domestic adversaries—especially tenured radical academics. In George Will's estimation, Lynne Cheney's was the more formidable foe.[37]

In her 1992 pamphlet, Cheney carries the culture wars to new heights by attacking the so-called politicization of the humanities, a development that she associates with the recent loss of faith by many academic leftists in truth, universality, objectivity, and disinterested inquiry. Cheney asserts, as if the notion were entirely unproblematic, that higher education should be about "trying to tell what is true." She rejects the "increasingly influential" view that truth is "merely a cultural construct, serving to empower some and oppress others."[38] In Cheney's view, those who espouse this conception are seeking to replace "truth with politics," a devious aim that Cheney regards as underlying post-structuralism, deconstruction, Marxism, and feminism.[39]

Cheney's discussion has a number of problems. First, she never qualifies or defends her view that the truth can be known objectively and impartially, and she never acknowledges the difficulties involved in mounting such a defense. Cheney, along with other critics of political correctness, seems remarkably uninformed about the tradition of skepticism that runs through the *philosophical* branch of the Western canon. The roots of philosophical skepticism about the possibility of discerning the truth, objectively or impartially, go back to pre-Socratic thought, and its champions have included that virtuoso of the Western philosophy canon, David Hume.

Some theorists believe that scepticism is incoherent because of being saddled with certain internal contradictions. A familiar criticism runs along the following lines: any assertions of the impossibility of truth, objectivity, universality, or the like only carry weight if they are themselves presented as true, objective, universal claims. If skeptics, however, present their own beliefs about the impossibility of truth as legitimate truth-*claims*, then they undermine their own assertions. The statement, "there is no truth," cannot be true without contradicting itself. It must, therefore, be false. Skepticism is thus refuted.

This criticism of skepticism, however, is very limited. If successful, it would undermine only an extreme skepticism that denies that *any* human assertions are true, including those of the skeptic herself. The refutation of extreme skepticism, however, does not establish that there is an objective, impartial truth to be discerned about any and every specific subject matter. That is, the failure of extreme skepticism would not establish that the truth-claims of, say, political or moral theorists were objectively or universally true. Philosophers are very familiar with qualified forms of skepticism; logical positivists, for example, reject the notions of metaphysical and moral truth while still championing scientific truth. A partial and limited skepticism that challenged a particular realm of study, such as theories of human sexuality or female nature, might succeed where extreme skepticism fails. The important point is that such limited skepticisms would not have to be formulated in self-contradictory or otherwise self-defeating terms.

A second problem with Cheney's portrayal of the academic left is that she ignores the diversity among different leftists. She treats varied leftists as if they comprised one monolithic group and then attributes to each of them the views about truth that only some of them hold. Most conspicuously, she treats deconstructionist critiques of the concepts of truth and objectivity as if this approach typified the views of all leftists, as if we had all abandoned faith in the possibility of discerning any objective truth whatsoever.

In the case of feminism, this characterization is false. Most feminists do regard knowledge as socially constructed, and for *some* of them, most notably postmodern feminists, this does involve a deconstruction of, and apparent loss of faith in, the notions of truth, objectivity, and the like. This postmodern perspective, however, is not universal among feminists.

Many feminists believe, for example, that feminist-oriented research in the social and natural sciences is better research, and therefore *closer* to objectivity and to the truth, than the traditional work it seeks to replace. Sandra Harding has carefully explored the views of those feminists who retain commitments to notions of truth or objectivity. Among these latter feminists are feminist standpoint theorists and those whom Harding labels "feminist empiricists."

Feminist empiricists accept the truth-seeking legitimacy of contemporary scientific norms and principles, and object merely to what they regard as bad science, science corrupted by sexist biases.[40] Feminist standpoint theorists attend to the social situatedness of knowledge-seeking practices, and believe that "women's situation in a gender-stratified society" provides epistemological resources that feminist research has harnessed and that can improve the quality of the search for knowledge. These resouces are thought to "enable feminism to produce empirically more accurate descriptions and theoretically richer explanations than does conventional research."[41]

Harding herself defends feminist standpoint theory, a view that for her requires a stronger notion of objectivity than do traditional, nonfeminist theories of knowledge. What is important about the requisite notion of objectivity is that it does not aim to be value-free.[42] Although this approach does not, in Harding's estimation, permit us to formulate an account of reality that is "absolute, complete, universal, or eternal," nevertheless it does permit us to provide explanations that are "less partial and distorted" than many of the accounts that knowledge-seeking traditions have handed us.[43]

Even those feminists who do raise questions about truth and objectivity do not always express a simplistic skepticism that is easily dismissed. The feminist epistemologist, Lorraine Code, proposes the view that "knowledge is, necessarily and inescapably, the product of an intermingling of subjective and objective elements."[44] Code's concern is to challenge the traditional subjective/objective dichotomy, which conceives of the subjective and the objective as "polar opposites" that mutually exclude each other, an approach that Code finds to be "implausibly simplistic." Code rejects the view that "knowledge is *better* to the extent that it is purely rational, theoretical, abstract, or universal." Code wishes to give both "subjective" and "objective" a "textured reading that can reveal their place in the situated experiences of cognitive agents."[45]

Code rejects a traditional conception of objectivity, but this is not the same as rejecting objectivity as such. Needless to say, nothing in Cheney's discussion shows a recognition of such intellectual subtleties. To be sure, I cannot say whether Code's approach is ultimately correct or workable. However, no particular account of the possibility of objective and impartial truth has convinced all philosophers either.

The third problem with Cheney's arguments is that she characterizes only cultural leftists as "politicized" while seeming to imply that those who proclaim a *faith* in the abstractions of truth and objectivity are, therefore, not politicized. This is an unwarranted suggestion. Those who proclaim a faith in truth and so on do not necessarily propound substantive views that are true, universal, objective, impartial, or politically unbiased. It is crucial to recognize that someone's views about the nature of truth can be differentiated from her other specific beliefs about the world. Someone might have the best available account of truth, yet still hold inadequate views about, say, sex differences in intelligence or the so-called discovery of America.

Faith in objective truth does not insulate someone's opinions about specific subject matters from possible distortion by political influences. The real problem does not lie in the concept of truth in its pristine abstraction. The real problem is to discern which of the many competing accounts of debated subject matters shall be deemed the truest account—and who shall be deemed the authoritative accountants to handle the books. It does not take a feminist to recognize that even if a universal, objective, impartial truth lies out there waiting to be discovered, nevertheless, we are finite, limited, partial beings whose claims to have discerned that truth may always be distorted by our limitations as knowers, including our political biases. As feminists and others have become increasingly aware, a loud endorsement of truth, universality, or objectivity is one of the most seductively effective rhetorical strategies for *masking* a biased perspective on substantive issues. Those who proclaim a faith in truth are not necessarily those who have discerned more of it.

Cheney constrasts the pursuit of "truth and objectivity" with the promotion of a "political agenda." My point is that this is a false dilemma. Those who declare themselves to be seeking objective, universal truth may have no less of a political agenda than those who raise skeptical questions about this or that area of human inquiry. Thus, Cheney fails to notice the political agenda that underlies her own concerns about higher education. At one stage, she implies that *democracy* is threatened by epistemological skepticism. "How can a *self-governing people* survive," she asks, "if they reject even the possibility of objective standards against which competing interpretations and claims can be measured?"[46] Like Kimball, in his defense of the Western canon, Cheney supports an objective conception of truth by appealing to its contribution to the survival of our democracy—a clearly political appeal to national interest.

The only stance that Cheney grasps as politicized is that which criticizes Western society and its history. In Cheney's estimation, political activists are those who exaggerate "the flaws of Western civilization" while making "other societies and cultures . . . seem fault free." This is another false characterization if applied to feminists. Although U.S. feminists continually reconsider the soundness of their cross-cultural critiques, nevertheless, U.S. feminist writings at one time or another have certainly criticized, say, clitoridectomy in Africa, the veiled life of women under fundamentalist Islam, suttee and bride-burning in India, and foot-binding in China.

In addition, if it is political to exaggerate the flaws of Western civilization, then it is just as political to underestimate them. Much multicultural and feminist literature is precisely an attempt to counterbalance traditional disciplinary work, which underestimated, overlooked, and even self-righteously excluded the concerns and perspectives of women, certain U.S. minority groups, and non-Westerners.

Cheney describes the "turn toward politics" as a movement toward "orthodoxies" that simultaneously discourages "the clash of ideas."[47] However, it is precisely multicultural and feminist literatures that challenge *traditional* orthodoxies, such as the uncritical glorification of America the beautiful. It is multicultural and feminist literatures that introduce a much-needed rethinking of those traditional ideas, and in so doing, sustain that crucial strand of the Western tradition: the spirit of free and open inquiry.

Antifeminist Backlash Reconsidered

Feminist women have become the females we all love to hate. They are the schoolmarm surrogates of the nineties, at whom we defiantly aim our verbal slingshots. Nasty fictional characters, such as *Fatal Attraction*'s Alex Forrest, conveniently reinforce the stereotypes that rationalize widespread feminist-bashing.[48] And why not bash feminists? For over two decades, feminists have been challenging deeply rooted conventions of social and cultural life. Surely it is time to strike back.

Mass media promote stereotypes that make it easy to ridicule feminists. The media caricature of a feminist hates the family, hates men, and hates sex.[49] She is a belligerent shrew or a whining victim (depending on what the audience most detests), yet she has clawed her way to the apex of professional power. Virtually omnipotent, she has caused every contemporary U.S. ill from the collapse of the family to the decline of global economic preeminence.

It seems as if many people have a perennial need to belittle some group of women or another, to make some women the targets of witch-hunts and the brunt of comic routines. If we did not have feminists to hate, we would have to draft some other category of women into scape-goat service. Women in general should be grateful to feminists for shielding them from the wife- and mother-in-law-bashing that used to be a cultural pastime. ("Family values," perhaps?)

Although academic life is supposed to be a domain that cherishes careful reflection, the attacks by some academics on feminism are often

no less caustic and no more reasoned than the feminist-bashing found
in mass media. These attacks are unfortunate. Academic feminism and
the interdisciplinary field of women's studies grew out of social movements aimed at improving women's lives. Feminist theory seeks an understanding of social and cultural life that can illuminate the ways to
diminish the exploitation, abuse, and oppression of women and to promote varied forms of female flourishing. Frivolous attacks on feminism
can only serve to undermine the energy and motivation needed to sustain these important social projects. The cost of suppressing feminism
will be the loss of real improvements in the lives of many women.

What are some of the improvements that the feminist movement has
struggled to achieve? They include ending workplace discrimination
against women; increasing women's participation in government and
economy; securing women's reproductive freedom; reducing violence
against women; combating the multiple oppressions of minority
women; fostering a female-centered eroticism; achieving equal rights
for lesbians; curtailing the sexual objectification of women; diminishing
women's economic vulnerabilities; eliminating cultural misogyny; correcting the scientific misunderstandings of women's health, physiology,
and psychology; promoting honesty about marriage and mothering; and
ending the sexual exploitation of women.

Academic feminism reflects this wider social movement by making
women's perspectives central to the development of knowledge. Feminist theory, research, and teaching are thus connected to the world outside the academy and to many of the social and political conditions of
that outside world. This connection is the basis of the frequent accusation that academic feminism is political. In the multiculture wars, this
charge is one of the most common complaints used to discredit feminism. Is academic feminism, however, *inappropriately* political? What,
in any case, does "political" mean in this context?

"Political" has become such a widely used epithet that it is difficult
to keep track of its meaning. The issues are confused when "partisan"
is interchanged with "political." The word "partisan" is often used in
the United States to refer simply to an allegiance to either the Democratic or the Republican party. Academic feminism is decidedly not
political in this sense.

If being political means being about government and public policy,
then much of academic feminism is indeed political—but so is most of
political science and substantial portions of economics and history. If
being political means being about power in social relationships, especially hierarchies of power, then academic feminism again is often po-

litical—but so, too, are much of political science, economics, sociology, history, and literature.

Roger Kimball throws some light on the sort of politics that is supposed to be illegitimate in the academy. Kimball accuses the Yale women's studies program of proclaiming that "sexual, racial and ethnic politics should . . . determine . . . the curriculum."[50] Kimball is here paraphrasing a passage in the Yale college bulletin of 1988. His paraphrase, however, misrepresents the Yale bulletin. The passage in question actually asserts, first, that a full understanding of society requires investigating women's experiences, and, second, that, toward this end, women's studies makes gender a "fundamental category of analysis." Thus, investigating women's experiences and making gender a fundamental anaytical category are what Kimball regards as inappropriate politics in the academy. This approach, he declares, is "deeply at odds with the presuppositions of traditional humanistic study."[51]

Kimball gets one point right. Traditional humanistic study did ignore the experiences and perspectives of women and neglect the full significance of gender in human life. That limitation, however, is a vice and not a virtue of traditional humanistic study. It is curious that so adamant a champion of universal interests as Kimball should fail to recognize the universal importance of gender.[52] The interest in gender seems as global as any interest can be; it, therefore, ought to be a prime analytical category for humanistic study. The historic neglect of it is an embarrassment rather than a point of honor. Furthermore, if taking account of women's experiences is another part of what being political means in academic life, then "political" shows its true colors as a term of high praise.

The sort of politics that feminism's critics want to expel from the academy appears to be the sort that aims at changing social conditions, practices, or institutions. In this sense, academic feminism is often political—but so, once again, are numerous other areas of academic study. Economics includes studies aimed at preventing economic cycles of inflation and depression; sociology includes studies aimed at alleviating poverty and reducing the crime rate; medical science includes many studies that aim at the prevention of disease by exposing the social conditions and human practices that make us sick. A great deal of research in medicine, physical science, and social science would never be undertaken or receive its share of scarce research dollars but for the prospect that the resulting knowledge might transform social conditions to people's benefit.

Thus, there is nothing inherently illegitimate about research that is guided by goals of social or political change. Nothing about the abstract idea of a commitment to social change intellectually invalidates in advance any research area or project inspired by it. Change-oriented commitments to liberalism, conservatism, libertarianism, socialism, and all the rest certainly shape many of the intellectual questions that we ask and motivate our interest in answering those questions.

The only social commitments that are legitimate candidates for exclusion from academic life are those whose acceptance would necessarily undermine the academy itself and its open forum for the consideration of ideas—Nazism, for example.[53] Despite, however, the familiar caricature of the intolerant "feminazi,"[54] feminism does not close down the public forum of ideas, but, rather, enlarges it by insisting that it include women's voices. True, some individual feminists are personally intolerant of views that they regard as clearly wrongheaded and dangerous for women. More often, however, it is feminists—tolerant as well as intolerant—who find themselves harassed and slandered by their own adversaries. Feminists have no academic monopoly over intolerance. Far from it.[55]

As with any of a person's loyalties, a commitment to feminism might bias a scholar's research methods or conclusions. Biases of any sort constitute a potential problem; they might lead a researcher to create research samples that are unrepresentative for the topic under investigation, or to suppress data that does not support the researcher's prejudices. Such distortions tarnish the quality of research and should be eliminated wherever they occur. These problems, however, are scarcely unique to feminist-inspired research.

Indeed, feminism has distinctly challenged numerous biases that permeate the research methods and paradigms of traditional disciplinary research, biases in favor of men and male points of view and against women and female points of view. In research on moral development or heart disease, for example, it seems obvious that the sex of the subject could make a decisive difference to the problem being investigated.[56] Yet prior to feminist critiques, women were routinely excluded as experimental subjects from such research projects, despite the obvious relevance of the research to both genders. Feminist empiricists, to use Sandra Harding's phrase, pioneered the method of exposing such antifemale biases.[57] Thus, the political nature of academic feminism, with its wider social agenda of ending women's subordination and promoting their well-being, has led to a substantial reduction in the gender biases that clouded traditional research practice.

Academic feminism's political nature is acceptable in another light as well. As I observed earlier, the strongest defense for the primacy of the Western literary canon construes that canon as serving a political role. The well-being of our society, so it is argued, depends on an educated citizenry that is acquainted with the most profound ideas expressed in European and Euro-American literatures. Traditionalists believe that it is necessary to teach the foundational principles of liberal democracy in order to preserve our own "liberal democratic polity." Traditionalists about western civilization often have a clear political agenda for the academy: bolstering national security. Feminist academic work as well as the Western canon thus both share, with many other areas of academic study, the commitment of supporters who believe that something of great value in the world at large hinges critically on the academic prominence of the studies that they, respectively, champion.

Moreover, among those wider social agendas that may legitimately guide academic research, the aim of improving our culture is no less appropriate a goal than that of preserving society's extant traditions and customs. No one supposes that our governments, economies, families, or media are already perfect or ever were. Research into these aspects of society and culture will provide the greatest benefits for us if they enable us to improve our social practices. Improvement includes preserving what is good along with bettering what is bad. To say, therefore, that academic feminism is political because it aims at certain transformations of social and cultural life is not by itself to have offered any reason for expunging feminism from the academy. Academic work regarding imperfect realms of human society and culture should always be open to the larger aim of social improvement if it is to merit the support of society's scarce research dollars.

In calling for a citizenry schooled in the principles declared to be the foundation of our government, traditionalists display their confidence in the capacity of those principles to promote the common good. By contrast, feminists and multiculturalists tend to believe either that our society has not always lived up to its founding principles or that its founding principles are limited in the extent to which they ensure the well-being of all people. According to this latter view, the common good requires the well-being of all the major groups of people within society. This achievement depends, in turn, both on diminishing the cultural oppression that many people experience by virtue of gender, race, or other group identities, and on promoting due respect for these differences at the individual and institutional levels. Both traditionalists and multiculturalists, including feminists, thus have a conception of what is needed to promote the well-being of our society, but the conceptions differ. Surely the academic curriculum can accomodate *both* perspectives.

Transforming the curriculum to incorporate women's experiences and the significance of gender improves the curriculum on its own terms. We do not need to locate ourselves outside academic traditions in order to recognize that the consideration of women's experiences (as understood from their own perspectives) and the serious attention to gender (an indisputably foundational feature of our social life) add up to better research. The result is an enrichment of intellectual inquiry into human life. It is absurd to suppose that the humanities or social sciences could possibly achieve an adequate understanding of human concerns without attending to the perspectives of women and without recognizing the social or cultural primacy of gender. Academic feminism thus corrects research and teaching in our culture.

So why all the fuss? Why is feminism under attack if its value is so great?

One of the striking features of the current campaign against feminism is its anti-intellectual slant and the fact that much of the war is being waged in mass media where a flair for glib wisecracks and an eccentric personality can score more points than thoughtful analysis.[58] The consumers of mass media are busy with their own lives and do not have the time, energy, or inclination to check out the relevant sources.

Even the prominent academic critics of feminism often rely on a popular style of rhetoric that avoids genuine scholarly dialogue and invokes antifeminist attitudes through the use of media stereotypes and buzz words. These critics extend their denunciations well beyond feminist views to encompass the professional behaviors and personality traits of individual feminists.[59] Many of the most prominently featured critics of feminism are women, some of whom even claim to be feminists of some sort or other.

Camille Paglia is an illustrative example. *Time* recently dubbed Paglia "The Bete Noire of Feminism" and celebrated Paglia's "contempt for modern feminists" which, *Time* unabashedly admitted, has "drawn the media with magnetic force."[60] It is Paglia's personal insults against feminists that seem to attract journalists the most. (Germaine Greer is a "drone," Diana Fuss's output is "junk," the feminists concerned with date rape are "sex-phobic, irrational, borderline personalities."[61]) Without the empty epithets, Paglia's actual criticisms of feminism are rather pedestrian—with a few bizarre exceptions. One such exception is this recent rebuke: "Feminism, with its solemn Carrie Nation repressiveness, does not see what is for men the eroticism or fun element in rape, especially the wild, infectious delirium of gang rape.''[62] Perhaps this sort of admonition is what Harvard government professor Harvey Mansfield, Jr., had in mind when he hailed Paglia's "fearlessness," her tendency to say "what you're not supposed to" and "tell off the boss.''[63]

Just who is this sex-phobic boss, blind to the delights of gang rape, whom the critics are so busy telling off and why is everyone so worried about her? The stereotypic feminist, we may recall, hates the family, hates men, hates sex, and commands an awesome degree of social power and professional might. What truth is there to this caricature?

Let us consider the family issue. Some critics of feminism castigate feminists for their hostility to "the" family, a concept that the critics often interchange with "the traditional family," and "the family as we know it.''[64] Since these notions are far from equivalent, the attack on feminism courts confusion from the start. The traditional family is what social commentators usually have in mind when praising "family values.'' The traditional family is a nuclear family consisting of a legally married heterosexual couple and their children, in which the man is the principal breadwinner and head of the household and the woman is responsible for all, or nearly all, the domestic work and child care. As early as 1977, however, this family form comprised only 16 percent of all U.S. households, according to the U.S. Census Bureau.[65] The traditional family, it seems, is no longer *the* family or the family as we know it but is only one sort of family that we know.[66]

A family is, generically speaking, any group of persons who together form a household based at least partly on some sort of enduring interpersonal commitment. Legally or religiously sanctioned marriage is one example of such a commitment but it is not the only one possible nor extant. The concept of an enduring household captures the core idea of family life, and it has the credibility of having appeared in dictionary definitions of "family" even before the recent wave of the feminist movement.[67]

The notion of an enduring household does not resonate with greeting card sentimentality, however, and that is its distinct theoretical advantage. The point of the conception is to serve as an analytical category to enable understanding of the institution. To understand contemporary families in their diversity, we need a generic concept of family life that does not presuppose any norms about who is supposed to do what. Family norms should be debated as separately as possible from the relevant descriptive categories.[68]

Defining family generically as any enduring household based on interpersonal commitment allows us to acknowledge the familyness of all sorts of domestic relationships. We already know (although some of us mindlessly forget) that families by adoption are genuine families and, thus, that biological links between parents and children are not necessary for family life. It is now high time to give social recognition and support to families comprised of heterosexual couples who are not married (with or without children), heterosexual couples who do not abide by traditional gender roles in domestic tasks or child rearing, lesbian and gay couples (with or without children), and single parents with children.

Any stable and nonoppressive domestic relationship will constitute a better family environment if it is, in turn, sustained by a respectful and supportive community that grants it all the privileges of family life, such as inheritance rights and access to affordable family health insurance. It is precisely by neglecting the needs of the many nontraditional families that our society is now at risk of forsaking family life.

Feminists work for the social legitimation of *these* families, which sadly still receive substantially fewer of the privileges reserved for traditionally correct families and which suffer a great deal of social stigma instead. In supporting nontraditional families, feminists promote family life more extensively and more thoroughly than their opponents who otherwise intone family values. Feminists, thus, do not oppose family life as such. Far from it. They are just as concerned as anyone else that the familial dimensions of our lives and our various enduring domestic relationships satisfy the needs and promote the flourishing of their participants—all of their participants.

When feminists criticize family life, their targets are usually male family dominance and the female dependency that it promotes and enforces. The traditional ideal family features a woman who earns no income outside the household and who, as a result, is economically dependent on her husband-provider for the satisfaction of her own basic needs and those of her children. Women in this position are more vulnerable than otherwise to abuse and exploitation by their husbands. They are, in addition, more likely to feel culturally devalued as housewives in comparison to their income-earning husbands who are socially defined by occupational status and by familial role as heads of household.[69] It is patently obvious that to criticize this form of family life is not to oppose family life as such.

It is also patently obvious that to criticize male-dominant families for the risks and oppressions that they harbor for women is not to criticize the women who choose such arrangements. Rather, it is to challenge uncritical and overly romanticized cultural representations of those male-dominant marriage and family forms. Women, depending on their circumstances, might well derive satisfactions within male-dominated marriages and families—but at what cost? The fact that some people are content with certain social arrangements is important information but not a conclusive reason to avoid questioning those arrangements.

Some theorists have, nevertheless, sought to undermine feminist critiques of the *male-dominated* family by suggesting unqualifiedly that such families are beneficial for women and that women secretly recognize this. Christina Sommers has written that women who avoid or get divorced from the male-dominated family "often" suffer harm and "might" feel "betrayed by the ideology" that led them to this state.[70] Sommers does not explain or support these vague warnings.

Alan Bloom is less reticent and more subtle in putting the point. Bloom has the candor to admit that the "old family arrangements" were not entirely good for women. He concedes that because of economic changes and the recognition of injustices, "the feminist case [against the old family arrangements] is very strong indeed." The problem, in Bloom's view, is that there are no "viable substitutes." Macho men can be "softened" but they cannot be made caring, sensitive, or nurturant. Men will make positive contributions to family life only in the old-fashioned families in which they can exercise power and protectiveness over "weak," "modest," "blushing" women (Bloom's words). Women's independence, however, diminishes men's motivations for staying thus married and providing for children. And women's premarital sexual independence reduces men's motivations for getting married in the first place. "Women can say they do not care," about this loss of men's interest in them, warns Bloom, "but everyone, and they best of all, knows that they are being, at most, only half truthful with themselves."[71]

This antifeminist theme has a cunning seductiveness to it. It avoids the argument that feminism is bad because it hurts men, an argument that, we must admit, will not necessarily deter women from joining the ranks. Bloom argues instead that feminism *hurts women.* If the very people who, out of direct self-interest, might be attracted to feminism can be convinced that feminism is bad *for them*, then there is some chance of stopping the spread of this contagion. The argument hinges on two claims: first, by becoming feminist (too independent, too self-reliant), women will lose male love and male commitment to marriage and family; and second, women *really want* male love and commitment more than they want independence—*regardless of what they might think.*

Telling women that feminism will hurt *them* is not a new tactic in the public debate over women's issues. Barbara Ehrenreich found examples of it written over two decades ago by Taylor Caldwell in John Birch society literature.[72] Caldwell argued in 1970 that, over the centuries, women had entrapped and hung on to men by both avoiding opportunities to earn their own incomes and feigning dependent personalities. By encouraging female independence, feminism threatens to undermine this "con." In the years since 1970, certain economic realities have made it harder to persuade women to give up their incomes. Bloom prudently ignores income but the rest of the argument remains unchanged: if women act too independently, they will lose male love and the opportunity for (heterosexual) marriage and family, which, Bloom says, they really want more than anything else.

This message evokes the age-old genre of cliches that warn women not to be too sensible or too self-reliant in their habits. After all, "men don't make tracks for girls who wear slacks," and "men don't make passes at girls who wear glasses" (an admonition that, in the days before contact lenses, required a woman to give up clear sightedness as a condition of pleasing men).[73] Since our cultural traditions give so little public recognition or esteem to love and friendship among women, the threat of a woman's being unloved by a man has the public meaning of being unloved period. What women, other than lesbians, would not be made a little anxious by these sorts of messages?

Perhaps I am merely expressing a tedious feminist attitude when rejecting the Bloom line. Perhaps it is my contempt for men that leads me to do so. This brings us to a second feature of the familiar caricature of a feminist: she is a rabid man-hater. Christina Sommers has argued that feminism promotes resentment toward men. Feminism, she claims, views society as a sex/gender system that divides people into a victim class (women) and an aggressor class (men). In terms of this framework, feminism rationalizes "wholesale rancor" by women against their aggressors.[74] Sommers rejects the concept of a sex/gender system and cannot abide resentment against men.[75] What can be said about her repudiation?

First, feminists in general do not promote an attitude of resentment against individual men unless those men, as individuals, abuse, exploit, or oppress women (as rapists, batterers, harassers, misogynists, etc.). A great deal of feminist theory is devoted to analyzing institutions and practices as social wholes, along with their characteristic male biases and the individual men who rise within them to positions of power and authority. This sort of analysis is hardly identical to promoting resentment against all individual men.

Also, some men enjoy, exercise, and promote "male privileges" a good deal less than do other men. Feminists recognize these differences (often based on race and class identities) and modify their reactions accordingly. In addition, many feminist women feel a solidarity with profeminist men who challenge male-biased and male-dominated social practices.[76] It is thus obvious that glib generalizations about feminists (number unspecified) promoting resentment against men (number unspecified) misrepresent the facts of the matter.

Second, the charge that feminists resent men ignores the focal point of feminist concern. Women, and not men, occupy the centerstage of feminist attention. The failure to recognize this shift in attentiveness exemplifies the same male-centered bias of our culture that feminism has always sought to contest.

There are at least two major dimensions to feminist concern for women. One dimension involves women supporting women. The early feminist notion of "sisterhood" reveals this aim. Feminism seeks to promote women's support, care, nurturance, respect, and esteem *for women*. Another dimension of feminist concern for women lies in the feminist challenge to social institutions and practices by which (some) men are enabled to dominate women (along with other men) and most aspects of social and cultural life.

In order for women to focus their energies, loves, and loyalties on other women, they must usually redirect some of their attention and support away from men.[77] As women begin to value and cherish each other more, their interest in men in general, and most men in the particular, inevitably declines. Women who are intensely focused on other women might ignore men altogether. Women also sometimes get angry at men who oppose the legitimate improvements that women seek for their own lives. In addition, women who spend time challenging male-dominated social institutions often become less reverent toward, even overtly critical of, the male achievements and authority buttressed by those institutions. At what costs were they achieved? Whose domestic service made them possible? To what ends have they been put? and so on.

Women's withdrawal of support for men, growing indifference or anger toward them, and overt criticisms of male-dominated activities are sure to be experienced by many men as hostility and resentment. Women's challenges to systems of male authority and power are also likely to be regarded as personal affronts by many men, especially men who benefit as individuals from those cultural systems. Some men—and even some women—are unable to regard these shifts of female attention and support as anything more than negative attitudes toward men, and are incapable of recognizing any positive value in women's redirecting love or support toward other women.

That interpretation, however, distorts the social changes in question and perpetuates the very problem at issue. It presumes that "profemale" means nothing more than "antimale," and that the only significant interpretive framework for assessing women's lives lies in their relationships to men and men's activities. To grasp that "antimale" is really a misnomer for "profemale" apparently requires a gestalt shift that exceeds the capacities of many social critics. Or perhaps some social critics are dimly aware of what profemale does mean, and it is precisely the reasonableness of this attitude that they are reluctant to concede.[78]

Third, even if feminism does foster genuine and positive resentment against men, this attitude is only a problem if it is unjustified. Is it unjustified? An affirmative answer requires a convincing case that women are *not* significantly exploited, abused, oppressed, or subordinated by individual men or by male-dominated social practices or institutions. This argument is not likely to be forthcoming soon.

My dictionary defines resentment as "anger and ill will in view of real or fancied wrong or injury."[79] Ill will is often a useless emotion, like spite or malicious envy, and may hurt most the one who feels it. No feminist wants women merely to reverberate with feelings of useless malice. Anger, however, can empower someone to harness her energies into positive action against the constraints that harm or oppress her. It is scarcely improper for feminists to want women to harness their energies into constructive action against the wrongs that are inflicted on them.

John Stuart Mill regarded as natural the feeling of resentment and the desire to retaliate against those who harm us. This attitude, in Mill's view, becomes properly moral when imbued with social concern, that is, when we thereby take ourselves to be standing up for the interests of society and "asserting a rule which is for the benefit of others," and not simply ourselves. It is this complex sentiment that, in Mill's view, sanctions no less than the rule of justice.[80]

Whether or not resentment toward men is justified depends in part on whether or not the wrongs or injuries that feminists think men have inflicted on women are real or merely fancied. This issue is not settled simply by complaining that resentment is not a nice attitude. To decide whether or not women are justified in resenting men, we would have to consider a wide array of social practices: unwanted male sexual aggression (including rape, incest, sexual harassment), economic discrimination against women, woman-battering, and so on.

It does not require much perceptiveness to see that women are at least *sometimes* wronged by men. It also does not require much historical knowledge to see that complacency has not helped women to end or to rectify those wrongs. In the United States, prior to the days of recent feminist anger, there were few places of refuge or support for battered women or rape victims; sexual harassment was not even a named problem; unwanted pregnancies could not be ended except by criminal and often life-threatening means; government and the economy were almost exclusively male-dominated domains, and on and on. The recent gains in women's social conditions have depended largely on feminist activism. Feminist activism, in turn, has been motivated, energized, and empowered by a variety of attitudes, among which anger figures prominently. Resentment against men would not be too high a social price to pay if it empowered some women to diminish their subordination to men and to promote their own well-being at long last.

Fourth, it might seem that feminists incorporate hostility against men into the foundations of their theories of the ''sex/gender system,'' the conception of society as divided into male aggressors and female victims, locked in endless antagonism. A sex/gender system (defined more carefully below) has to do with the host of societal differentiations that are based on sex or gender. Sommers, who criticizes feminists for using this concept, at the same time makes numerous claims specifically about women, claims that she does not generalize to men. She tells us, for example, just what women want (a man, children, clothes that render them sex objects, etc.), and she defends women's, but not men's, choice of the traditional *social* roles of wife and mother, roles that have been reserved exclusively for women.[81] Yet Sommers denies that there is such a thing as a sex/gender system. Some clarification is obviously needed.

A sex/gender system, in general, is a certain type of social system. It is an orderly interrelated whole comprised of social phenomena pertaining to sex and gender. More carefully still, a sex/gender system is an interrelated system of practices that differentiates persons based on their sex or gender, the differentiation having implications for the identities, roles, norms, values, ideals, expectations, and so forth that pertain to those persons.

There is no doubt that most, if not all, human societies feature a sex/ gender system of some sort. The institutions of sexuality, marriage, child rearing, productive activity, military defense, and governing, in most human societies, allocate roles partly according to gender. In addition, most human societies sustain these wide-ranging roles with a host of child rearing and other practices that promote in females and males the personality traits and identifications appropriate to their adult gender roles. The real issue is not whether we have a sex/gender system; obviously we have one.[82] The real controversy has to do with its precise nature and the extent to which it benefits or disadvantages women.

Feminists have construed the particular sex/gender system of the United States as one of pervasive male dominance and female subordination. This specific view of the sex/gender system in the United States is one that we can debate. To argue intelligently against this view, however, calls for careful reconsideration of a good deal of evidence in its favor.[83] Even if the thesis of a male-dominant sex/gender system does manifest feminist resentment against men, the truth or falsity of that view is independent of such resentment and should be debated on empirical grounds.

Fifth, and finally, even if some women are now directing negative, nasty, useless resentment toward men, that issue would be trivial in comparison to the gender-related difficulties still facing women, difficulties ranging from economic barriers to sexual violence. Most men can handle a few sneers. The problem of resentment against men is a triviality that does not deserve our further attention.

The third and last stereotypical feature of a feminist is that she hates sex. First note the subtle tension between this accusation and the charge that feminists oppose the family. Sexual extravagance hardly meshes well with traditional family values. The sex devotee is in for a rude awakening when she tries to maintain a life of carnal delights on an exhausting schedule of round-the-clock feedings. The time and energy required to raise children with the attention they need competes with the time, energy, spontaneity, and freedom required by a devotion to sexual excess—except, perhaps, for those who enjoy the privileged services of nannies and housekeepers. Marriage even without children usually fosters monogamous expectations that dampen, if they do not suppress altogether, the polygamous sexual enthusiasms that many people would like to pursue.

Of course, ''sex-phobia'' is not the only alternative to sexual profligacy. There is ample room for moderated sexual indulgence in a life also dedicated to family, friends, and other valued pursuits. Feminists, however, raise the same sorts of embarrassing questions about male domination in the context of sexual practices that they do regarding male domination in family life. To call this feminist reaction ''sex-phobic'' is to assume, rather remarkably, that sex without male domination is impossible.[84] And to ridicule feminist cautions about sexuality is to manifest a mindless sexual libertinism.

Unfortunately, sexual libertinism has yet to face the sexual crises of the 1990s. We are a culture deeply confused about sex. We live in a world so burgeoning with population that some commentators already warn of imminent brutal, militaristic, global anarchy.[85] We live in an era when individual sexual contact can be a death-defying act. Eros has become Thanatos. We bemoan, in one breath, the problems of rampant teenage pregnancy, global overcrowding, and sexually transmitted diseases, yet, in the next breath, scold feminists for their prudery. Go figure.

Amidst all this sexual chaos, the antiseptic notion of informed consent offers some individual and local guidance. Informed consent is a person's most important right of self-protection against the serious risks posed by sexual contact. Informed consent, however, must be genuine. The image of Rhett Butler dragging Scarlett O'Hara up the stairs despite her protests for some sexual brutality at his but not her instigation is a sad anachronism.[86] Even when no coercion or pressure is involved, a woman has not given informed consent unless she has both a clear understanding of the risks involved and the genuine option of protecting herself against those risks with prophylaxis and contraception—or refusal. If it is sex-phobic to say so, then perhaps our culture needs more sex-phobia.

We can no longer afford to view with tolerant amusement the glorification of male sexual aggression or the myth that women in general enjoy it. Apart from the question of women's right to protect themselves against risky sexual contact, the idea that women in general enjoy sexual domination is, to say the least, perplexing. It is an odd psychology that would see no need to explain why someone enjoyed being dominated or humiliated, sexually or otherwise, and a still odder sociology that would unquestioningly attribute this phenomenon to whole groups.

The societal conditions that could promote and explain female sexual masochism are not hard to find. Typical patterns of gender socialization combine with mass media, advertising, and other cultural institutions to feed us a steady diet of messages that glorify and eroticize male sexual aggression and male sexual domination of women. Mass media and advertising compound the problem by relentlessly urging women to shape their sexuality around pleasing men—in their appearance, behavior, and sexual responses.

Critics of feminism might charge that this analysis is patronizing (matronizing?) toward women. That facile response, however, would be off the mark. For one thing, it is not only women, but men as well, whose desires are affected by socialization and cultural images. For another thing, an entire advertising industry is built on the conviction that media images and messages do significantly impinge on human desires. Are advertisers really just wasting our time and their financial millions? While the research is often inconclusive and the notion of strict determination overstates the case, nevertheless, numerous studies reveal complex effects of mass media on people's attitudes.[87] Why suppose that women would be immune to these influences or that it would not affect one of the most plastic of human passions, sexual desire?

Media portrayals of heterosexuality that endorse, routinize, and eroticize men's domination of women and women's deference to men are the key problem. How we solve the problem is, of course, an open question. Nothing about feminist critiques of those media entails the view that individual women—or even, with more reason, men—should be "forced to be free." I am not, that is, advocating that anyone be legally denied her pound of pornography or put through nonconsensual sex sensitivity training. Cultural dialogue about the issues is the preferred feminist approach. The cultural dialogue about sexuality is obstructed, however, when feminists who criticize male-dominant heterosexuality are condemned by Paglia as "sex-phobic" and by Sommers as totalitarian "Big Sisters" out to enforce "boring" "sexual correctness" on innocent women.[88]

When sex can lead to unwanted pregnancy or a fatal disease, it ought to be obvious to everyone that no one should be pressured to engage in it and no one should be denied an informed understanding of what is going on. Women should have full and genuine control over their sexuality. This has been a feminist credo from the start. Media representations of male sexual conquest, no matter how titillating to some consumers, glorify nothing less than women's loss of sexual control and consequent inability to protect themselves in a crucial realm of their lives. Sexual correctness, or, more carefully, heterosexuality without male domination, may offend the sensibilities of some, but the gain in women's control is well worth the cost. And when it comes to sexual pleasure, only a sadly limited range of experience or a failure of imagination could warrant Sommers's insistence that sex minus male domination is "boring."

Sommers herself vacillates between two different defenses of male-dominated sexuality. On one hand, she denies that various scenes of it are really domination at all.[89] Yet, on the other hand, she mounts an apologetics of sorts on behalf, for example, of the "fascination" felt by women (number unspecified) for the scenes in question and for domineering male characters like Rhett Butler.[90] The two lines of thought work at cross-purposes. If it is not really domination, then there is nothing to absolve and the defensive tone is inexplicable. If it is really domination, then the possibility that some women like it should not undercut our critical reflection on the practices in question. We, as a community, can still ask ourselves whether we want to continue supporting cultural glorifications of women being coerced, pressured, or seduced into sexual encounters over which they exercise no control.[91]

When a woman is "locked" in a man's embrace, she may become aroused by the "bonds" of love and want the sexual contact to continue. Her compliance under those conditions, however, is hardly the sort of self-protective, informed consent that she needs these days for her own safety. The precipitous urgency of sexual arousal does not by itself provide any reason to trust a man's assurance at the time that, yes, he had a vasectomy and, yes, he is HIV-negative.[92]

Sex is no longer just a playful pastime and the means of reproduction; sex has become a matter of life and death. *It ain't the '60s anymore.* Sexual (as well as nonsexual) images of men dominating women and women submitting to men have always been insulting to women. In the 1990s, they represent a dangerous frivolity we cannot afford.

Political correctness: academic malignancy or educational salvation? My discussion has ranged over speech codes, the Western canon, multiculturalism, apolitical truth-seeking, and feminism. I did not endorse speech codes, but I did find that some opposition to the codes amounts to a covert attempt to silence leftist speech. I did not advocate the overthrow of the Western canon but I did call for it to be counterbalanced by deep multiculturalism. I did not reject the ideal of objective truth but I did argue that truth-seeking is a practical matter that cannot be guaranteed apolitical. And I did defend feminism, by disputing the antifamily, antimale, antisex caricature that substitutes for reasoned criticism of feminist views. In each case, I have sought to vindicate some of the politically correct ideas and practices that are currently revolutionizing academic life.

Notes

1. My essay deals mainly with political correctness in U.S. postsecondary education. Many of these same issues, however, seem relevant to other Western nations.

Political correctness encompasses a variety of viewpoints, ranging from very moderate to very extreme. It is important for the critics of political correctness to engage with the most defensible versions of it; otherwise they are not giving the perspective its due and are deceiving their audiences. Thus, I do not pretend to represent the whole gamut of politically correct ideas; instead, I offer what I regard as the most reasonable versions of feminism, multiculturalism, and the rest.

2. *UWM Post v. Board of Regents of the University of Wisconsin System*, No. 90-C328, Oct. 11, 1991. See also Michele N.-K. Collison, "Hate Speech Code at U. of Wisconsin Voided by Court," *The Chronical of Higher Education* 38, no. 9 (1991): A1, A37.

3. *R.A.V. v. City of St. Paul* (1992) 112 S.Ct. 2538.

4. *Chaplinsky v. New Hampshire*, 315 U.S. 568, 569 (1942), at 571–72.

5. Rodney A. Smolla, *Free Speech in an Open Society* (New York: Alfred A. Knopf, 1992), p. 162.

6. Christopher Shea, "Court's Decision on 'Hate Crimes' Sows Confusion," *The Chronicle of Higher Education* 38, no. 47 (1992): A26–27.

7. Nat Hentoff intermingles his criticism of formal speech codes with examples of students who wanted to criticize, say, affirmative action but did not do so because they feared the wrath of intolerant leftists (" 'Speech Codes' on the Campus and Problems of Free Speech," in *Debating P.C.*, ed. Paul Berman [New York: Dell, 1992], pp. 217–18. Reprinted from *Dissent* [Fall 1991]). Hentoff's juxtaposition erroneously makes it seem as if speech codes themselves contribute to this supposed repression.

8. Martha Albert Fineman, "Who Pays for Free Speech?," *Women's Review of Books* 9, no. 5 (1992): 17.

9. For an argument that such codes are appropriate, see Stanley Fish, "There's No Such Thing as Free Speech and It's a Good Thing, Too," in *Debating P.C.*, ed. Berman, pp. 231–45.

10. This problem does not show that the arguments against the codes are logically flawed. It pertains instead to the sincerity of code critics.

11. The gag rule was upheld by the U.S. Supreme Court in *Rust v. Sullivan* (1991) 111 S.Ct. 1759. That one particular group of U.S. Supreme Court justices decided the case in a particular way in 1991 does not mean, of course, that the issue is not further debatable.

12. Cf. Hyman Rodman, Betty Sarvis, and Joy Walker Bonar, *The Abortion Question* (New York: Columbia University Press, 1987), p. 137. According to these authors, the percentage of support among U.S. adults for the availability of legal abortion varies with the circumstances of the pregnancy. In case of danger to the pregnant female's health, pregnancy due to rape, or strong chance of fetal abnormality, a strong majority (89 percent, 81 percent, and 79 percent, respectively) approved of abortion in a 1985 survey. Other reasons received less support; for example, only 40 percent of those surveyed in 1985 approved of abortion for a married woman who simply did not want any more children.

However, an astonishing 36 percent (more than one-third) of those surveyed approved of abortion "for any reason."

13. Someone might argue against my analogy that there is a significant difference between a salaried employee and a consumer of a service. Workers at federally funded health care clinics are partly salaried by the federal government and are, therefore, like employees who are paid partly out of tax dollars. Students, by contrast, are more like consumers of a service. One could argue that there is no basis for regulating the speech of those who merely consume a service, even if the service-providers do not like the speech, but that an employer has a legal right to withhold the salary of an employee who speaks in a manner that the employer does not like.

As mentioned in the text, however, it is doubtful that even a majority of the U.S. taxpaying population would have agreed to support the gag rule, had they been asked. Lack of "employer" unanimity in this case makes the employer-based argument of questionable relevance.

Rodney A. Smolla is one opponent of campus speech codes who also opposed the abortion gag rule. He argues that the government should not be permitted to attach, to the receipt of its funds, conditions that "brazenly prefer one set of ideas over another," and thus accomplish indirectly the "viewpoint discrimination" that is supposed to be precluded by the guarantee of freedom of expression (*Free Speech*, pp. 216–19).

14. Hentoff, " 'Speech Codes,' " pp. 218–19.

15. *Ibid.*, pp. 221, 224.

16. Roger Kimball, "The Periphery v. the Center: The MLA in Chicago," in *Debating P.C.*, ed. Berman, pp. 62–64. Reprinted from an earlier version in *The New Criterion* (February 1991).

17. *Ibid.*, pp. 69, 74; italics in original.

18. *Ibid.*, pp. 64–65.

19. *Ibid.*, p. 65.

20. William Bennett, *To Reclaim a Legacy: A Report on the Humanities in Higher Education* (Washington, D.C.: National Endowment for the Humanities, 1984).

21. *Ibid.*, p. 30.

22. Donald Kagan, "Western Values Are Central," *New York Times*, May 4, 1991, p. A23.

23. Allan Bloom, *The Closing of the American Mind* (New York: Simon & Schuster, 1987), p. 4. That these accusations faintly echo the fatal charges against Socrates—corrupting the youth of Athens and blaspheming the city gods—is an irony that seems to have been lost on Bloom.

24. A third argument also sometimes appears in the debates. This is the contention that the Western canon comprises those works of the West that have been found to have surpassing aesthetic merit. I omit this argument from my discussion, but some of my responses to the universality of the canon argument are relevant, by analogy, to answering it.

25. Kimball, "The Periphery," p. 64.

26. This point is made by John Searle, "The Storm over the University," in *Debating P.C.*, ed. Berman, pp. 94–95. Reprinted from *New York Review of Books*, December 6, 1990.

27. Multiculturalists have raised important questions about the presumed "we" whose intellectual heritage is identified as Western. Henry Louis Gates, Jr., for example, has observed that "we" in the United States really have a diversity of intellectual heritages that are "our own," but that only an Anglo-Saxon culture has been counted as the "common culture" ("It's Not Just Anglo-Saxon," *New York Times*, May 4, 1991, p. A23).

28. Kimball, "The Periphery," p. 82.

29. There is a danger that this remark will be misunderstood. First, I am not saying that anything and everything is political. This common caricature of leftist belief is not a meaningful claim. My view is this: the defense of the Western canon in terms of its necessity for sustaining our liberal democracy presupposes a particular sort of political commitment no less than does the perspective of most defenders of multicultural studies.

Second, a political commitment or bias does not necessarily preclude someone's gaining insight into truth from such a perspective. If people differ widely in their political commitments, however, it is unlikely that they will agree on what the truth is.

30. Cf. Sara M. Evans, *Personal Politics: The Roots of Women's Liberation in the Civil Rights Movement and the New Left* (New York: Knopf, 1979); and Sara M. Evans and Harry C. Boyte, *Free Spaces: The Sources of Democratic Change in America* (New York: Harper & Row, 1986).

31. See, for example, Dinesh D'Souza, *Illiberal Education: The Politics of Race and Sex on Campus* (New York: Random House, 1991, 1992), pp. 73–75.

32. *I, Rigoberta Menchu: An Indian Woman in Guatemala*, ed. and intro. by Elisabeth Burgos-Debray, trans. Ann Wright (New York: Verso, 1983). D'Souza discusses this book in *Illiberal Education*, pp. 71–73.

33. D'Souza, *Illiberal Education*, p. 72.

34. Clare McKeown, "Rigoberta, Nombre de la Paz," *Oxfam America News*, Fall 1992, pp. 1, 4.

35. Paula Rothenberg's *Racism and Sexism: An Integrated Study* (New York: St. Martin's Press, 1988) took center stage for a while in the multiculturalist controversy after its defenders attempted to include it as part of their curricular reforms at several major universities. In this case, no international committee set its seal of approval on the work in question. See George F. Will's criticism of the book and the attempt to make it required reading in composition courses at the University of Texas at Austin and see Paula Rothenberg's response, both reprinted in *Debating P.C.*, ed. Berman, pp. 258–68.

36. Lynne V. Cheney, *Telling the Truth: A Report on the State of the Humanities in Higher Education* (Washington, D.C.: National Endowment for the Humanities, 1992).

37. George F. Will, "Literary Politics," in *Beyond P.C.*, ed. Patricia Aufder-heide (Minneapolis: Graywolf Press, 1992), p. 25; reprinted from *Newsweek* 117, no. 16 (1991).

38. Cheney, *Telling the Truth*, p. 7.

39. *Ibid.*, pp. 22–23.

40. Sandra Harding, *Whose Science? Whose Knowledge?* (Ithaca, N.Y.: Cornell Univ. Press, 1991), pp. 111.

41. *Ibid.*, p. 119.

42. *Ibid.*, ch. 6. This conception of objectivity might strike some as debatable. My point here, however, is not to debate the view in question but rather to show that the notion of objectivity does find a prominent use in feminist theory.

43. *Ibid.*, p. 187.

44. Lorraine Code, *What Can She Know?: Feminist Theory and the Construction of Knowledge* (Ithaca, N.Y.: Cornell University Press, 1991), p. 30.

45. *Ibid.*, pp. 28–30.

46. Cheney, *Telling the Truth*, p. 39; italics mine.

47. *Ibid.*, p. 45.

48. See Susan Faludi's discussion of the antifeminism in the Hollywood film, *Fatal Attraction*, and her general survey of media caricatures of feminist women in *Backlash: The Undeclared War against American Women* (New York: Crown, 1991).

49. I discredit these stereotypes later in this section.

50. Roger Kimball, *Tenured Radicals: How Politics Has Corrupted Our Higher Education* (New York: Harper & Row, 1991), p. 17. Kimball is referring to "Yale College Programs of Study," *Bulletin of Yale University*, ser. 84, no. 7 (1988): 123.

51. *Ibid.*

52. See the second part of this essay.

53. Stanley Fish argues that our legal system should, and indeed implicitly already does, take this sort of approach to freedom of expression; speech is not protected if it threatens to undermine foundational political institutions ("There's No Such Thing as Free Speech and It's a Good Thing, Too," in *Debating P.C.*, ed. Berman, pp. 231–45). As Fish notes, there have been substantial historical disagreements over which speech is foundationally threatening.

54. This expression was promulgated by radio talk show host, Rush Limbaugh; see his *The Way Things Ought to Be* (New York: Simon & Schuster, 1992, 1993), p. 194.

55. For an account of some of my own experiences as a target of antifeminist intolerance, see my letters to the editor in the *Proceedings and Addresses of the American Philosophical Association* 65, no. 7 (1992): 58–61, and 67, no. 1 (1993): 24–27. Examples of intolerance from other sources also abound. For example, I have attended several conferences funded by the Liberty Fund of

Indianapolis at which the few token Marxists and Keynesians invited to the events were roasted by the predominantly libertarian audiences.

56. For a discussion of the male biases that influenced work in the psychology of moral development, see Carol Gilligan's famous *In a Different Voice* (Cambridge, Mass.: Harvard University Press, 1981), e.g., pp. 18–19. For a discussion of the omission of women from medical research on heart disease and other generic human ailments, see Susan Sherwin, *No Longer Patient: Feminist Ethics and Health Care* (Philadelphia: Temple University Press, 1992), e.g., p. 166.

57. See Section III, at note 40.

58. One example is Rush Limbaugh's "Feminazi Trading Cards," with "all the vital statistics" on the back, including waist and hip measurements and "number of abortions" (*Way Things*, p. 204).

59. See, for example, Christina Sommers's accusations against "leading" feminist philosophers (and their responses to her accusations), which appeared in the *Proceedings and Addresses of the American Philosophical Association* 65, no. 5 (1992): 92–97; 65, no. 7 (1992): 55–83; and 66, no. 5 (1993): 99–108. The unprecedented publication, by the American Philosophical Association, of Sommers's professional misconduct accusations and character diatribes against named feminist philosophers raised embarrassing questions about the fairness of APA leadership at the time.

60. Martha Duffy, *Time*, January 13, 1992, pp. 62–63.

61. The first two of Paglia's insults are quoted by Duffy, p. 62; the third is quoted by Paula Chin, "Street Fighting Woman," *People*, April 20, 1992, p. 126.

62. Camille Paglia, "It's a Jungle Out There So Get Used to It!," *Utne Reader*, January/February 1993, p. 64.

63. Quoted by Chin, p. 129. Harvey Mansfield, Jr., is a current member of the advisory board for the National Endowment for the Humanities, having been nominated for that position in 1991 by then-director of the NEH, Lynne Cheney.

64. See Christina Sommers, "Philosophers against the Family," *Person to Person*, ed. George Graham and Hugh LaFollette (Philadelphia: Temple Univ. Press, 1989), pp. 87–88.

65. Cited in Barrie Thorne with Marilyn Yalom, eds., *Rethinking the Family* (New York: Longman, 1982), p. 5.

66. I have previously discussed this issue of definition in " 'They Lived Happily Ever After': Sommers on Women and Marriage," *Journal of Social Philosophy* 21, nos. 2 & 3 (1990), p. 57. Some scholars have recently challenged the presumption that the "traditional family" was *ever* as widespread as family nostalgia buffs would have us believe. See, for example, Stephanie Coontz, *The Way We Never Were: American Families and the Nostalgia Trap* (New York: Basic Books, 1992).

67. See, for example, definition #3 of "family" in the Funk & Wagnalls

Standard Dictionary of the English Language, International Edition (Chicago: Encyclopaedia Brittanica, Inc., 1965), p. 457. I have added "enduringness" to the dictionary definition in order to exclude transitory cohabitation arrangements.

68. One norm that feminists take pains to defend is the responsibility of adults to care for and nurture the children in their own family households.

69. See Susan Moller Okin, *Justice, Gender, and the Family* (New York: Basic Books, 1989), esp. ch. 7, "Vulnerability by Marriage." It is important to note that the so-called traditional family has neven been traditional for all social groups in our culture. Women from low-income households often worked outside the home long before the current wave of the feminist movement.

70. Christina Sommers, "Feminist Philosophers Are Oddly Unsympathetic to the Women They Claim to Represent," *Chronicle of Higher Education*, October 11, 1989, p. B3.

71. Alan Bloom, *The Closing of the American Mind* (New York: Simon & Schuster, 1987), pp. 129–32.

72. See Taylor Caldwell, "Women's Lib: They're Spoiling Eve's Great Con," *American Opinion*, September 1970, p. 27. Quoted in Barbara Ehrenreich, *The Hearts of Men: American Dreams and the Flight from Commitment* (New York: Doubleday, 1983), pp. 158–61.

73. The inequality of "men" and "girls" has still not disappeared.

74. Christina Sommers, "Feminism and Resentment," panel presentation to the American Association for the Philosophic Study of Society, Washington, D.C., December 28, 1992.

75. Christina Sommers, "The Feminist Revelation," *Social Philosophy & Policy* 8, no. 1 (1990): 152–57.

76. See, for example, Larry May and Robert Strikwerda, eds. with the assistance of Patrick D. Hopkins, *Rethinking Masculinity: Philosophical Explorations in Light of Feminism* (Lanham, Md.: Rowman & Littlefield, 1992).

77. Marilyn Frye articulates this notion well in *The Politics of Reality: Essays in Feminist Theory* (Trumansburg, N.Y.: The Crossing Press, 1983), esp. pp. 72–82 and 162–73.

78. Rush Limbaugh, invoking the common stereotype, brands "many" leading feminists as "manhaters" (p. 188). For him, this stance was exemplified in the controversial episode of the television series *Murphy Brown*, in which the lead character, Murphy Brown, a single woman, gives birth to a child and decides to raise it on her own. According to Limbaugh, "The real message of that *Murphy Brown* episode was that women don't need men, shouldn't desire them, and that total fulfillment and happiness can be achieved without men or husbands" (p. 189). To equate such a message with hatred of men is the error I am highlighting.

Limbaugh offers no arguments against the view that he derides, but it is obvious that some women indeed do not need men (or a man), should not desire them, and can very well achieve fulfillment and happiness without them.

79. Funk & Wagnall's *Standard Dictionary of the English Language* (Chicago: Encyclopedia Britannica, 1965), p. 1071.

80. John Stuart Mill, *Utilitarianism*, ed. George Sher (Indianapolis: Hackett, 1979), pp. 50–52.

81. I recount Sommers's views and provide citations to her writings in " 'They Lived Happily ever After': Sommers on Women and Marriage," pp. 57–65; the points cited in the text above are from p. 57.

Only the legal and social prohibitions against gay marriage prevent men from being able to be wives to other men. And apart from gestation and lactation, male biology is no bar to "mothering" children. There is nothing an adoptive mother can do for her child that an adoptive—or nonadoptive—father cannot do for his child just as well. Nevertheless, our society continues to differentiate parents based on their sex identity. This sort of practice is precisely what is captured by the notion of a sex/gender system.

82. More probably, we have a number of sex/gender systems, reflecting the privileges and constraints of other overlapping social groupings such as race, class, religion, and so on. Men of a socially subordinated ethnic group, for example, might be just as unlikely to hold the reins of governmental power as women of the same ethnic group. Interrelationships between those women and men might show less, or merely differently distributed patterns of, male domination than is found in white, middle-class U.S. culture.

83. Deborah Rhode has carefully documented numerous areas of male abuse or domination of women that have figured prominently in law; cf. her *Justice and Gender* (Cambridge, Mass.: Harvard Univ. Press, 1989).

84. Some feminists share this view but find it lamentable and not a cause for celebration; see Catharine A. MacKinnon, *Feminism Unmodified: Discourses on Life and Law* (Cambridge: Harvard Univ. Press, 1987).

85. See, for example, Robert D. Kaplan, "The Coming Anarchy," *Atlantic Monthly*, February 1994, pp. 44–46, 48–49, 52, 54, 58–60, 62–63, 66, 68–70, 72–76. Kaplan believes that the contemporary U.S. emphasis on multiculturalism is weakening the ability of the United States to withstand the impending militaristic disasters (p. 76). The alternative view, however, is equally compelling, namely, that genuine multicultural dialogue, where possible, is our only hope of forestalling mass destruction.

86. According to Margaret Mitchell's own narrative wording, Rhett was "bullying and breaking" Scarlett in the scene in question; he "humbled her, hurt her, used her brutally" (*Gone with the Wind* [New York: Macmillan, 1936], p. 940). For my more extended discussion of this scene and the novel in general, see "Does Sommers Like Women?: More on Liberalism, Gender Hierarchy, and Scarlett O'Hara," *Journal of Social Philosopy* 21, nos. 2 & 3 (1990): 85–88.

87. See, for example, Jennings Bryant and Dolf Zillmann, eds., *Perspectives on Media Effects* (Hillsdale, N.J.: Lawrence Erlbaum Associates, 1986); and Doris A. Graber, *Mass Media and American Politics*, 4th ed. (Washington, D.C.: CQ Press, 1993).

88. "Sex-phobic" is Camille Paglia's term; see note 14. "Big Sister," "boring," and "sexual correctness" come from Christina Sommers, "Argumentum Ad Feminam," *Journal of Social Philosophy* 22, no. 1 (1991), p. 12.

89. Regarding the scene in which Rhett "bullies," "breaks," "hurts," and "brutalizes" Scarlett (see note 40), Sommers rejects the word "rape" and resists even the somewhat milder notion of sexual domination ("Argumentum," p. 15). The producer of the movie, *Gone with the Wind*, was not so shy. David O. Selznick referred frankly to this scene as the "Row and Rape." See Helen Taylor, *Scarlett's Women: Gone with the Wind and its Female Fans* (New Brunswick, N.J.: Rutgers Univ. Press, 1991), p. 130.

90. Sommers, "Argumentum," pp. 15–16.

91. Sommers tries to convince her readers that feminists are out to impose totalitarian reconditioning on women, so as to make women's sexual desires conform to feminist blueprints (*ibid.*, pp. 11–17). To correct such distortions, it is necessary to state clearly that: (1) I criticize not the women (if any there be) who enjoy images of men dominating women, but rather the cultural endorsements and glorifications of male-dominated heterosexuality; (2) there is an obvious difference between merely criticizing a type of cultural representation versus actually forcing one's values and ideals on other people; and most importantly, (3) I do not seek to *impose* my values or ideals on anyone, but rather to share my views with others through dialogue and debate. Sommers's caricatures of feminist views threaten to shut down genuine dialogue altogether. By contrast, I offer reasons to support my conviction that male-dominated heterosexuality is disrespectful to women at best, and, at worst in the 1990s, positively fatal. My hope is that we, as bearers of culture, will alter our predominant values and diminish our consumption of those potentially disastrous images.

92. Women's second most likely source of contracting AIDS is heterosexual contact (with men who already have it), the most likely source being intravenous drug use. Women are also at much greater risk than men of getting AIDS through heterosexual contact alone. See Nora Kizer Bell, "Women and AIDS: Too Little, Too Late?," *Hypatia* 4, no. 3 (1989): 5. As ever, heterosexuality poses far greater risks for women than it does for men, at the same time providing insufficient intrinsic deterrents to male sexual aggression.

Politics, Ethics, and Political Correctness

Jan Narveson

Introduction: Politicization

Our subject is a contemporary syndrome—the not entirely homogeneous set of phenomena known as "political correctness." Intriguingly and perhaps significantly, this phrase, originally stemming from the bad old days of the Bolsheviks and meant, I suppose, to be cute and rather derogatory, has been embraced by its friends almost as readily as by its enemies. It's hardly to be taken literally: the tendency to refrain from assassinating adherents of rival political views, or of rival candidates for political office, is not to be so classified, even though it is political, certainly, and it is indeed "correct." There are good and strong reasons of principle for having and cultivating that tendency, but it is not the sort of thing designated by the expression "politically correct." That phrase was born to live between scare-quotes: it suggests that the operative considerations in the area so called are *merely* political, steamrollering the genuine reasons of principle for which we ought to be acting and to promote which, we hope, our political institutions are designed. Presumably the friends of political correctness could not accept that characterization. They surely suppose that the policies they advocate are defensible via broadly acceptable principles. In this, I think, they are wrong, and I shall try to make a detailed case for that in the following pages. The focus here, at any rate, is on principles and arguments—on the *conceptual status* of the policies we are considering.

There is one attitude toward subjects such as the present one to which, I think, objection should be made right away, and analysis of which will serve as a prelude to the rest of this essay. It is often enough said nowadays that *"everything* is political," or words to some such effect; and those who say that often invoke it in support of positions on currently controversial matters. I'm not at all sure how seriously the claim is made by those who make it, or what, if anything, they really suppose it means. But it might be worth opening this discussion by pointing out why the slogan can be no more than that—that insofar as one can attach any kind of serious meaning to it, the effect can hardly be what was intended by anyone purporting to provide *reasoned* support for any describable view on any discussable subject.

To see this, let us ask what would be the range covered by the word "everything" in our slogan? One supposes it applies at least to the realm of discourse generally, and of decision making in particular. Consider, then. Is the question *whether one proposition implies another* intended for inclusion? If it is, presumably the idea is that whether or not proposition q actually *follows* from proposition p is to be regarded as itself just as "political" as whether p is true in the first place. But if that is what is meant, then what is the point of invoking the slogan on behalf of any *particular* view, as opposed to other views? For if the question whether the view follows from the slogan, or from anything, is itself a political matter, rather than a matter of logic or fact, then there is evidently no way to know whether the slogan "supports" one view or another about anything, including politics itself. (Try it . . !) Like so many other similarly uninhibited generalizations, this one has a remarkable capacity for undermining itself: if it were right, then a political decision could suddenly make it the case that the very theory of political correctness is itself false. I presume that proponents of political correctness don't think that is so.

Everything's being literally political is unimaginable. In no useful sense of "political" can one hold that the question of, say, whether there is global warming, or Snell's Law holds up, is political. What it would properly apply to, for example, might be committee deliberations that are suspected of being influenced by political rather than scientific reasons to declare for a particular scientific judgment when some other judgment, or none, was actually better supported by the evidence. Perhaps, for example, more money would be available from the granting agency if one side in the issue was declared to be the right one ("If your research is intended to support hypothesis H, then we'll give you a research grant of twenty thousand dollars; if not, forget it!" A current example: the belief that HIV "causes" AIDS, despite much contrary evidence.[1]) In this perfectly clear and usable sense of "political," however, it is plainly false to say that "everything" is so. And it is also clear that the term is essentially pejorative in such contexts. If you do science by consulting political interests, that *impugns* your work as science: those who did such things should have their Ph.D.'s revoked and their labs turned over to people who will take the job seriously.

Why would anyone be tempted to suppose that "everything" is political? The argument seems to appeal to some such argument as this: (1) All judgments are formulated in words; but (2) words are social artifacts; and yet (3) society is political (because it has political institutions, which exercise control over it).

Of course we must grant all of those premises. But what conclusion are we supposed to draw? That molecular chemistry is really a branch of politics, perhaps? After all, its conclusions and reports of evidence are indeed written and spoken in some language. Or should we instead argue that politics is actually a branch of molecular chemistry, seeing that everything, including politicians, is composed of molecules? Better yet, the claim should be dismissed for the absurdity it is.

Nevertheless, the topic of political correctness is genuine enough. The claim that "everything" is political is used in practice to support a move *to politicize*, that is, to increase the incidence of political control in some domain that was not previously so treated. The argument we have just considered is readily seen to be nonsense. If its premise were correct, then whatever domain was in question must *already be* political, in which case there is no sense in proposing to *politicize* it. Its not having been literally so (or, as much so) in the past is an obvious presupposition of proposing to make it so, or more so, in future. On the other hand, if that presupposition *is* true, then the general covering premise is false—*not* everything is political. You can't have it both ways. But the argument requires precisely that.

Thus, the proponent now needs new, and this time *meaningful*, premises for supporting the proposal. And everything would turn on the plausibility of those premises. We can supply some meaning to the suggestion hat everything is political by interpreting it to mean that everything that anything can be done about is conceivably something that can be legislated about. But the fact that something *can* be done hardly means that it ought to be: everyone is capable of murder, for instance.

Politicizing means that instead of being free to do as they think best, people are now directed by some authority to do something else. It means, then, an increase in administrators and an increase in taxation or other impositions on somebody, or on everybody, to support the costs of the politicization. Above all, it means a decrease in individual voluntary deliberation and decision. IThese are all evils, in my view, to be avoided unless there is a much greater gain from the new measures, to justify the extra costs. My argument, in each case, is that there is in general no gain to speak of from these policies for anyone except, perhaps, the administrators themselves, and much loss for everyone else. All of them are made in the interest of ''justice,'' according to their proponents. But justice, as I will argue, is precisely what gets lost in the shuffle.

The Issues

Among the various issues clustered under the general heading of political correctness, I will discuss the following five:

1. Should there be ''canonical'' bodies of literature in various academic disciplines or domains? To suppose that there are, says political correctness, is to be racist, sexist, or in some other way discriminatory.

2. Should the study of this or that subject, especially in the humanities, reflect the multiplicity of cultures from which various contributors have stemmed? The politically correct view has it that the whole field should be reconceived so that various cultural expressions that have not hitherto been regarded as contributions to it are to be regarded as being so after all—and what's more, they get equal standing with the canonical ones.

3. What about concepts such as truth, objectivity, and impartiality? Is there anything left of them after postmodernism, in particular after applying the theory known as ''deconstruction''? The politically correct view is that those notions must go—or be given political interpretations.

4. What about persecuted and oppressed groups? Should they be given preference in academic (and other) hiring, or the distribution of related rewards or distinctions? Political correctness supports what is now known as ''affirmative action,'' supposedly to remedy the situation.

5. Finally, there are speech codes. Various spoken or written utterances are regarded as deprecatory or otherwise harmful when they previously weren't so considered, or perhaps made positively illegal when formerly they were regarded as minor matters that should be left to the persons involved. The political correctness view is that we should greatly expand the range of the notion of harassment, thus opening the doors to committees empowered to enforce politically clean talk.

These are all real issues in practice. In response to these questions, curricula have been revised, assorted cultural groups given various special privileges, speech codes and "zero harassment" provisions adopted, and hiring practices altered by requiring affirmative action on behalf of various groups (most prominently, women). And this is done on the basis of theories, ideals of what society should be like. Our question is whether those ideals and the theories underlying them are really acceptable. In each case, I argue, they are not. The basis for affirmative answers to these questions is lacking. On the other hand, there is ample reason for *not* doing the various things in question. Each involves in one way or another important losses to innocent people trying to get on with their lives.

The Theory of Political Correctness

It would be helpful if we could spot any common basis for the "political correctness" types of action in these domains. Do they actually have something substantial in common? Is there a single direction of departure from familiar norms that they all involve? There is indeed. They take shape as various applications of a single general idea. That idea and its associated principles form the fundamental subject of this essay, though my discussion mainly focuses on specific claims in the five areas identified.

The common structure that seems to me to be at work in all of these proposals is the pursuit of what is claimed to be *equality*. Individuals, firms, and associations have objectives, attainable in varying degrees by the exercise of skill and intelligence—especially the latter, in the academic cases concentrated on here. In the pursuit of academic ends, some people will be found who perform better than others, and those people are selected, in preference to others less talented, for positions in the institutions and associations working toward those ends. And in various other ways, too, they are recognized and rewarded more highly for their achievements. Yet political correctness takes the view that the ones who do less well, and who are correspondingly less rewarded by academic institutions, are being somehow cheated or mistreated. They are regarded as "oppressed," by that very fact, or because their lesser performance is claimed to be a manifestation of some other oppression, in the form of "domination" by some group: by the rest of us, say, or by the "winners" in the current arrangements, or by those who support them. It is then proposed that to rectify the situation we must do one or more of the following:

1. Alter the standards by which better and worse performance is appraised.

2. Create special avenues to the desired rewards, or to the attainment of higher levels of performance, for those who have hitherto done less well, thus smoothing the way so that they too will do better, as judged by the existing criteria.

3. Impose handicaps on those at the upper end of the spectrum, thus to some degree equalizing their situations as compared with those lower down.

The fundamental aim, in short, is *equality of outcome*, and the politically correct principle is that everyone has the right to that status, a right overriding any considerations of merit deployed within the offending field.

This analysis does not apply so readily to the fifth of the proposed topics. Even speech codes, though, may be viewed as attempts to equalize the situations of speakers and hearers in certain respects. The kinds of speech objected to are viewed as manifesting a kind of domination of the hearers by the speakers. Speech codes are meant to restore equality between them.

The case for these efforts at equalization depends on either a reassessment of the objectives of the field, or a claim that the standards employed in appraising efforts on behalf of those objectives are in some way objectionable—say, that those standards or even the objectives themselves are really the creations of the allegedly oppressing class, whose members get to define them. That some such move is essential to the program is clear when we reflect that the possibility of achieving objective truths about the subject matter in question is an intrinsic presupposition of the academic endeavour at hand. Inquiry, as we used to understand it, proceeds by patient tracking down of evidence that tends to support some hypotheses in preference to others, sometimes to the complete epistemic exclusion of some of the latter, and to support them quite independently of what the inquirer might *like* to be the case. Human intelligence does the sleuthing, but nature itself confirms or disconfirms the answers. So long as that assumption is made, there are objective criteria of achievement, and it is hardly surprising that some do better and some worse, and thus that reasoned claims can be made about who should be preferred to whom for the purposes of that field of inquiry.

If you don't like this situation, one way to deal with it is to accuse those in the upper performance brackets, or their friends, of rigging the whole show, thus reconceiving the activity in question as mere power-tripping on the part of a self-appointed elite. Such an accusation must be taken seriously, for as we have seen, all non-political correctness theorists will agree that if that is what is actually going on, then our efforts at what we thought was objective science or scholarship are mere pretensions. The accusation, in fact, amounts to asserting that the subject in question is not really a *subject* at all, but just *politicking*. Aristotle is replaced by Machiavelli as the patron saint of the academic.

Political correctness advances these claims on the basis of more or less plausible-sounding premises. None of us approves of injustice or unfairness; all of us favor, in some sense, equal treatment of all. If those familiar principles can be brought to bear in these areas with the effects in question, then how can we object?

But in all this there is a mixture of ideology and misunderstanding. The latter is, I shall argue, extensive. Like all misunderstandings, especially those that drive ideologies, there are important truths on which the argument tries to build—but it builds in the wrong direction, leaving a theoretical jumble and leading to practical nightmares. The ideology involves a moral vision. But it is not what it claims to be. It is, instead, a flawed vision—actually *ressentiment*, in the guise of critical "theory." That is what I shall argue for in the ensuing pages.

The Canon

We begin with the idea of there being a *canon* in some domain of the humanities: a smallish set of works that constitute the paradigms of achievement in that area, the works one must know if one is to qualify as an educated person. Or, since almost all of the attention in this area has been concentrated on works in the broad area known as the "humanities," acquaintance with the canon qualifies a person as educated in the humanities—though that is pretty near to being the area that many people would identify with being "an educated person," period.

This calls for specific comment. There are plenty of people with impressive knowledge in non-humanities areas. Yet in their areas, "canons" are largely out of the question. Scientists read Newton and Galileo only out of historical curiosity, not as useful sources of knowledge in their subjects. I shall say more about the ideal of a "liberal education," an ideal that still seems to me important. Insofar as there is an ideal of education for all, of the educated *person* as opposed to the paleontologist, economist, biochemist, etc., the ideal of a liberal education in the humanities is at its heart. But let us not delude ourselves into supposing that such persons are the intellectual aristocracy of our time, or that it is everyone's sacred obligation to acquire such an education.

We will suppose, then, that it is in the area of a liberal humanistic education that there arise questions about the legitimacy of any "canon" of masterworks or paradigm works, regarded as a "core," basic to the subject. That said, let us begin by agreeing that there is plenty of unclarity and imprecision in the idea. It would be silly for anyone to claim to know *precisely* how many items really are canonical in any given humanistic area. Moreover, the areas differ greatly. Are *all* the works of Jane Austen in the canon, or just one or two? If the latter, is it, then, *Pride and Prejudice*, or *Emma*, or some other? Is George Eliot in the canon, or is she on the fringe? Faulkner? Virginia Woolf? Who would ever seriously advance *precise* claims about the canon? Among serious scholars, surely, the very idea of a precise list is laughable. Even if asked to name the ten most important works in the field, let alone the top hundred, most teachers and scholars of the subject, however eminent, would submit quite different lists.

Nevertheless, lists of that kind will also contain many common entries. Indeed, it is that very fact that gives the idea of a canon such credibility as it has. Very few will put Shakespeare far down the list. None will elevate the novels of Benjamin Disraeli (sometime Prime Minister though he be) to the top. Anyone who would seriously support an opposite classification would have to be written off as just out of it. But that is, in its place, an important fact. It is certainly this level of agreement that makes the idea of a "canon" a workable one. Without it, the idea couldn't get off the ground. There would then be genuine doubt on the validity of the field as a field: if the supposed knowledge and the supposed standards of this field are worth their salt, surely its practitioners would be able to agree enough to distinguish the best from the mediocre?

That said, some important qualifications are in order. First, it is not right to say that the canon consists, simply, of the *best* works in the field. We must instead speak, more guardedly, of important works: e.g., because they are seminal—as having inspired further work, and worthy of our interest for having done so, even if successors improved on them. Still others are recognized for certain special qualities, even though in other respects they would not be held up as models. There are flawed masterpieces, brilliant but eccentric works, minor masterpieces, small gems, and so on. The canon, in short, is bound to be a somewhat unruly collection. That should go some way toward dispelling any aura of sanctity about it.

What grounds might there be for attacking the very idea of a canon? To formulate these, we will have to be a bit more elaborate in our depiction of the idea. I have spoken, vaguely, of the objectives of a field, by reference to which we may identify better and worse practitioners within it. But how do we do that? We must be able to say more precisely what this or that person has accomplished—what it is about his or her work that makes it better. Thus we require a distinction between the general *objectives* of the field, on the one hand, and the *criteria* in terms of which meritorious performance is to be appraised, on the other. We shall then need to make a further distinction: between those criteria, which are the abstract categories within which appraisals are made, and the *standards* in terms of which we express and categorize particular appraisals. Standards indicate levels of achievement on the basis of the criteria in question. Thus in awarding grades to papers, we use such criteria as clarity, depth, and acquaintance with the relevant literature; and we then sort them into those meriting "A," "B," "C," and so on. In a body of literature, we look for imaginativeness, perceptiveness, delineation of character, and many other things; and we rate the various works as first-rate, second-rate, and so on.

But how do standards and even criteria come to be recognized in a field? People do not usually carry such things about in their heads when they look at works of art or read literature. Or at least, they do not have them in explicit form. It is safe to say that fields in which such appraisals are made tend to be based on reactions to particular works upon acquaintance, *not* formed *on the basis* of antecedently formulated criteria of appraisal. Having tried it and liked it, intelligent and interested people begin to figure out what it was that they liked about it, and perhaps reflection about that enables them to go on to further work, and sometimes to rethink the unreflective judgments themselves. Here is one main lead-in to a canon, then: the accumulation of items in the field that really catch and hold the interest and admiration of those interested in that sort of thing, and that do not undergo revision at the hands of further reflection and continued acquaintance with those and other works. Such works come to be looked up to, and to set standards: "A good philosopher, though no Aristotle," we say.

All the factors mentioned have to work together. If there are no objectives, then there are no criteria of appraisal; and in the absence of those, it makes no sense to call anything a "standard." A standard *for what*, we ask. In the case of many of the humanities fields in academia, it would not be very easy to say what the "objective" of its literature is. What is the purpose of a novel or a poem? We might say, taking a shot at it, that it's to be interesting, insightful, inspiring, to show us something about ourselves, and so on. Those descriptions of objectives, though, are obviously not informative enough to give anything like precise guidance. Seeing how some particular work measures up will itself require an exercise of insight, sensitivity, and taste: it won't be possible to say, "And there, you see, this is precisely what makes this poem fulfil that objective to such-and-such a degree."

For similar reasons, it is not easy to specify the goal of an academic teacher and/or student of literature. The very specification of goals is done in terms of value judgments. To those who have no feel for the field, this fuels the suspicion that it isn't really a "field" at all, and this in turn supports the political correctness analysis. Contrast this with, say, chess or many branches of engineering. The object of the chess-player in a game is very precisely specified: to checkmate one's opponent's king. Strategies are extensively studied, but they all have that single, clear, perfectly-defined objective. Whether x is a good move or not, though often debatable, is frequently decidable. And "canonical" practitioners are identified: Bobbie Fisher (in his prime) was a great player, whereas I, for example, am a very rank amateur. There is no real room for argument on the latter examples. Anyone who thinks that I, for example, am a "great" player has either mistaken me for someone else, or simply doesn't know what's going on in the game of chess.

But the case against the humanities fails for the same reasons. Take the case of this author (or, probably, yourself) as a pianist. With work, I just might be able to pass a first grade examination; with much more, I might someday get as high as grade four. But to mention me in the same breath with an Ashkenazy would be absurd. On the other hand, rating Ashkenazy as compared with Rubinstein or Perahia would be much more difficult. Luckily, it is also unnecessary for most purposes. If one were selecting recordings to play for a class, or for a group of music lovers, one would then have to make such choices; but one would be able to explain, usually, that other choices could also have been defended, that selection is to a degree arbitrary, and to a degree a matter of personal taste.

Why evolve a canon for purposes of teaching in college literature courses? For one thing, it is quite natural. People in the field read not only what they are assigned as students but very much else as well. Competent students of a body of literature read far beyond the confines of any canon: most of what is read, indeed, is by definition not in it. This puts them in a position to make informed judgments about relative merit, and those judgments tend, as a matter of fact, to converge on a modest body of works, which consequently are dubbed "classics." In undertaking to explore a field with a group of students, with limited time at both the teacher's and their disposal, a selection must be made. It makes sense to include some of the acknowledged best of the type under consideration. It also makes sense to include seminal works, the ones that have actually stirred up creative juices among authors. And it makes sense to include some work that is *not* the "best," for comparison.

All this is, I hope, boringly familiar. Given the aim of teaching, it is hard to see how one could proceed very much differently. And in any case, there is plenty of room in a sizable college or university for other courses in which specialties are pursued, or in which there is a deliberate choice to look at some of the less-than-best, and so on. The question, then, is whether there is anything basically wrong with the procedures described—this being the political correctness thesis about canons. But the question is unintelligible unless we have some idea what's going on in the body of works considered, and have absorbed enough of it to be able to recognize and present relevant criticism. Given that, it is possible to criticize the critics: to say, for instance, that what this one says is wildly irrelevant or wrongheaded or biased. But it is not so easy to do the same for the entire corpus—to say that the whole field is wrong from the start, somehow. Is it, indeed, possible at all?

The Canon and the Aims of Education

Obviously, there is a major problem here. To attack this question, we must ask what the aims of education are. But of course, we will then recognize right away that those aims are very diverse, and legitimately so. Some students avowedly aim merely to increase their eligibility for specific types of employment, and many parts of many universities cater to them. Others have visions of how life could be, for themselves or society—visions of varying degrees of clarity, and varyingly clear or fuzzy ideas about what will help to realize those visions. Still others are there for no particular reason—or even "just to get an education." It is especially the latter that interest us here. But it is important to appreciate the aegis under which we proceed. There are conceptions of education *as such*, of "the educated person," which deserve our attention, perhaps deserve everyone's attention, even though they do not have the status of that to which all citizens may be required to submit. The old but not dead idea of a *liberal education* may be acknowledged to be something of a specialty—a very different kind of specialty from, say, electrical engineering. It is what especially brings up questions about cores and multiculturalism. Let's have a look at notions of cores in the light of such ideals.

I take it that what makes an education "liberal" is, roughly speaking, that it hopes to be synoptic, to include a liberal dose of everything, or some approximation to that. The liberally educated person is supposed to be *widely* educated—to have a more comprehensive view of what there is to know. Such a student aims to know something about everything, though not, obviously, in minute detail. And at the top of the list of what such a person needs to know—especially nowadays—is that it is impossible to know everything, and thus that one must settle for knowing merely *something*, though the idea is for it to be something that has a bearing on the project of general knowledge.

A very large part of the liberal education will consist of studies concerning people: via the social sciences, from psychology through economics and sociology, and especially via the humanities, from the arts, literature, philosophy, and religious studies. If one hopes to achieve the general view, the broad reach, the nontrivial, beneath-surface understanding of the extent of human knowledge, how will one best do it? In part, surely, by attending to what is regarded by one's predecessors as the best, most important, most fundamental, and most innovative.

Well, is that sensible, or is the whole idea a mistake? Perhaps it does not, in a sense, matter. There are many colleges and universities, many programs of diverse kinds in any given one, and in any case it is perfectly possible to get through life without having gone to one at all. Universities are a luxury, not a necessity. Or in any case, what they are necessary for, if so, is the living of lives that humans can and very often do do without—lives of thought and reflection, stimulated by exposure to literature and art, and enabled by a broad knowledge of science and human affairs. Many have accounted themselves happy despite lack of those amenities, and plenty who have them have failed to be happy. In fact, it would be utterly unreasonable to insist that everyone *must* benefit from university education. There are people whose skills, talents, or interests simply do not lie in that direction; for them, academic life would be confining, frustrating, and irrelevant. One should not wring hands over that. It really does, as they say, take all kinds. (One of the things a liberal education would, I hope, teach, is precisely how *stupid* it is to have contempt for the "uneducated.")

Even so, we would have to worry if the whole idea of "liberal" education is a non-starter. If it is thought that there is not, because there *cannot* be, knowledge of that kind, then it would indeed be game over for the liberal aspiration. But why wouldn't there be? The biologist in her laboratory in Manhattan certainly knows more about the rainforest, in many respects, than the people who live in it. She may have had all her training in English, her teachers may all have been WASPS, and yet here she is, with a sizable body of hard facts, plausible and more or less confirmed hypotheses, and a confirmed capacity to find out more. But just the same is true about, say, Renaissance logic or Grecian urns. There are people who *know* quite a lot about these things. To suppose that fanciful Cartesian-style doubts undermine those achievements is to go very far off the rails. The proofs of puddings are in eatings, and academia, including its departments of humanities, offers a plentiful feast for those willing to check it out.

In short, universities and colleges exist and flourish because there actually is something for them to do. *What* they do is, to be sure, inherently "elitist": it is not for the noncurious, nor for the dim of intellect. But for all those capable of acquiring general knowledge, there is no real problem in establishing that there is a great deal of human knowledge to be surveyed, considered, digested, and added to. Nor is there any problem, for them, in seeing that its very existence, and the possibility of progress in future, depends upon the existence of broadly learnable rational procedures, canons of inquiry. In learning them, one develops discernment, including a sense of what is and what isn't of major significance in the field of inquiry at hand. The world of knowledge is an ample one. How, then, could there be any reasonable doubt that exploring it at a general level is a coherent aim? Where there are particulars, there is scope for finding universals, general properties of and connections among the particular.

Western civilization, to be sure, is not a "subject," but a vast tapestry of human happenings and experiences. In studying or thinking about it, we mostly study its emanations, especially its literary and artistic ones. That certain writings have been, over the millenia, very influential among thoughtful people is hardly surprising, and to recommend those to contemporary students as promising avenues to the achievement of at least some understanding of this large part of the world around us makes eminently good sense. (The objection that it is only a part of that world will be considered in the next chapter.)

Political correctness, in its extreme form, supposes that the "canon" is simply an arbitrary construction by some privileged elite. What would we need to do to refute this claim? First, we would have to suppose that the substantial measure of agreement among those acquainted with the fields in question is either just an accident or the result of some sort of collusion. The first alternative would be the decisive one, as I have agreed—but is too implausible to be worth considering. But if it is the latter, then what sort of "conspiracy" would we be talking about? Simply *saying* that there is a conspiracy at work is hardly enough. One would have to explain the motives of the supposed conspirators, in a credible way that also shows why they should be identifying not only some list or other, but the particular lists they do, as the "standard of the industry."

Finding a plausible way to do this won't be easy. Scholars in the humanities are a diverse lot, united in little but their common love of their fields. Moreover, they will be able to tell us quite a lot about these works, pointing to salient felicities and insights. Those who wish to pull down hallowed statues are going to have to *do better:* they will have to convince us that they have alternative bodies of work that are equally or more credible. If in an occasional case they succeed at this, well and good: it will then be added to the canon, which is, after all, an open-ended list. But they will almost always fail. For anyone who knows enough to be able to mount such a case is also most unlikely to be inclined to mount it. The canonical items are durable because, frankly, they do have the qualities claimed for them: close acquaintance is likely to persuade the serious reader or listener.

The most popular version of a conspiracy theory has it that the canon is the work of white males. Why there would be such a conspiracy, especially in the academic world, is an interesting question. And why on earth it would work the particular way it evidently would have done is especially mysterious. Male students of English literature admire Jane Austen, Emily Dickinson, Virginia Woolf: how did these women come to be so admired if there is a conspiracy to keep the literary world masculine? In general, the problem with any such hypothesis in this area is the same as the problem of giving a rational account of discrimination in hiring, which we will be exploring later: scholars have no obvious reason for rejecting work of quality on irrelevant grounds, whereas they do have obvious reason for not doing so: they enjoy literature. And there are obvious explanations for the modest incidence, in times past, of literary and artistic work by women. In ages—all, until recently—when virtually all women had perhaps ten pregnancies in a lifespan much shorter than our present ones, and no modern conveniences to reduce the toil of domestic work, few had the sheer time for it. In the contemporary world, by contrast, the productivity of women in scholarly and artistic areas is far greater, as one would expect from the enormous reduction in demands at home, and increase in life expectancy. And what they write is read with pleasure and enlightenment by others of both sexes and all races.

The case for the canon, then, is a broadly empirical one, even though the whole field is shot through with judgments of value. Sophomores may insist that value is, in some pejorative sense, "subjective," which of course is true, in the elementary sense that it involves reactions of feeling and taste. But it simply does not follow that anything goes. And an enormous amount of experience shows that it doesn't: literary and artistic canons reflect shared experience, both extensive and prolonged.

Multiculturalism

Having argued that the idea of a canon, broadly speaking, makes sense, given the aims of a liberal education, we now need to confront a recent challenge: the claim that such things as lists of classics are culturally biased. It is worth pointing out, to begin with, that the extent and intensity of this complaint is a mark of liberal institutions at work. Persons of diverse culture, religion, ethnic background, and race intermingle in Western countries whose doors have been more or less generously open to immigrants (and, in the case of the United States, considerably populated with the descendants of involuntary "immigrants" in times past). Thus we come to our second question: whether and how the literary and humanistic studies, at least, ought to reflect this greater multiplicity of cultures. Has the liberal society now generated a serious problem for itself?

Here the possibilities listed at the outset become acutely relevant. Canonically recognized works of English literature have been written by persons of foreign descent, including immigrants, and by non-Caucasians as well. Moving to nonliterary works, the inclusion of artists of all the sizable ethnic and racial groups of the world would likewise be confirmed—and by the normal standards, those supporting the familiar canons, rather than by specially rigged ones designed to let a few token outsiders in.

Yet the complaint we are considering here is such that those familiar facts would be regarded as mere sops, reflecting failure to confront the true significance of cultural multiplicity, and especially as politically motivated failures to do so. The nature of the new challenge is radical, insisting that the prominence of, say, Caucasian males on any such lists of great books (or whatever) is itself sufficient to testify to the biased nature of the criteria that generate those lists. Current demands for recognition of multiplicity call for an apportioning of the canons on the basis of the cultures from which various contributors have stemmed, say in rough proportion to their numbers. And/or, the thesis is that the fields of endeavour in question must be reconceived so that practices not hitherto regarded as contributions to it at all really are so after all.

In considering a charge like this, we need to distinguish carefully between the two different components of this charge: on the one hand, that it is cultural, and on the other, that it is biased. Of these two the first is, of course, obviously true; but the second does not follow at all from the first. Claims of bias are subject to objective evidence: one must *show* that what is so called is due to an irrelevant influence. When made both specific and relevant, as it must be to have any force, we will find that it is neither sustained nor sustainable at the level of generality required. In fact, it seems clear that those who make it simply infer from the fact that literary and artistic judgments are made from within some culture to the conclusion that they are biased. Once one appreciates that it simply doesn't follow, the case collapses.

Every book is written somewhere, by an author who was born and raised somewhere, speaks some language, and was exposed to and participated in some more or less identifiable cultural practices. It usually reflects that culture as well, sometimes so much so that it becomes a major source of our knowledge about the culture it came from. With this in mind, what are we to make of the charge that the Western canon is biased? The argument, as I say, seems to be that if it is culturally specific, it is *therefore* "biased." Well, why? And how?

The understandings of people within a given culture may well be biased on certain subjects. Their standard stock of information, or their standard patterns of reaction to many phenomena, might make them simply fail to consider some alternatives, dismissing them without argument if mentioned at all, or finding them simply unintelligible. Aristotle's defense of slavery comes to mind as a case in point. Having come up with impressive reasons why the whole phenomenon of slavery should have been regarded as outrageous, he nevertheless accepts it, and rather lamely defends it, without much awareness that there might be something just a teensy bit off in his assumptions about slaves. O.K.: But is there any similar reason for doubting the wisdom of Aristotle's theory that virtues are such as to admit of two contrary vices, or that syllogisms in AAA form are valid? Does somebody have a reasonable account of how *those* theses might be said to be "biased"? Or to take another, this time quite trivial case, Jane Austen's admiration for the navy, apparently prompted by the fact that members of her own family were naval officers, may be classified as a bias. But does any knowledgeable reader deny that Austen's portrayal of the limited range of human character traits that she does concern herself with are sharp, perceptive, and witty? I suspect not. But proponents of charges of general cultural bias should do so, after all. In fact, they *owe* us an account of that. 'Bias' is a term with genuine meaning—not one to be simply kicked around like the proverbial football. And that meaning is such as to require recognition and judgment on the basis of what *is* relevant: only thus can we in some cases judge that someone's motive in making a certain judgment was *not* so.

When we come to an entire curriculum at a liberal arts institution, we have a problem on our hands. What is the aim of such a curriculum? Only if we have a handle on this can we plausibly judge that its selection of means to that end is unsatisfactory in some way, e.g., that it is biased by inadequate recognition of multiculturalism. (In saying all this, by the way, I reflect an academic bias. There are, of course, plenty of nonacademic contexts in which the question of how to take proper account of multicultural phenomena could also be raised.)

In fact, a good case may be made that a liberal education should, in the first place, explore and consider works that emanate mainly from the culture in which the particular institution operates, and in the second, that it should try to make students aware of the existence of many different cultures, and of the respects in which they may sharply diverge from one's own. They should attempt to acquaint the student to some degree with sample ideas and artifacts from alien cultures. I take this to be a commonsense desideratum, and one that is taken seriously in typical liberal arts curricula. In typical cases, it may be true that a bit more along that line would be advisable. But 'a bit more' is not what the political correctness proponent has in mind.

What, then, *does* he or she have in mind? The most extreme version of the idea would call for "equal time" for each distinct culture: the proportion of literature in the liberal arts curriculum from one culture as compared with any other would, say, be roughly in porportion to the size of their relative populations. If there are any who seriously contemplate such a proposal, they would have to be asked how they propose to *count* cultures—to come up with at least a rough criterion for where one "culture" begins and another leaves off. If they've done their homework, there'll be a minimum of at least several hundred. They should next tell us *how much* time they have in mind when they talk of "equal" time: two minutes each, in a one-term course? Ten seconds? The scantest reflection in this direction confronts us with the absurdity of the proposal. When Herb London, of the National Association of Scholars, suggested that "there is not enough *time* in the school year for what Asante wants," Molefi Kete Asante responded, "Of course there is—if there is enough for the Eurocentric information, there is enough time for cultural information from other groups."[2] Asante seemed content to divide all the relevant groups into precisely two: Europe and Africa. No mention of China, India, Latin America, no interest in differentiating among the dozens of distinguishable cultures in Europe, let alone in Africa or all those other places. A modest amount of arithmetic shows the aptness of London's comment. Considering the relative sizes of Chinese and Indian populations compared to African, one suspects that Asante would not have been very happy with the result if we took his proclaimed "equality" seriously: the African texts would scarcely be mentioned in a truly equal-time agenda. And if we switched from a population-based criterion to a criterion based on quantity of literary production, the result would be far worse, from his point of view.

Having appreciated the need to retreat from any serious claim to equal time, the question now arises where the multiculturalist is to stop—and, of course, *why*? There can hardly be a nonarbitrary answer, a fact that itself may imply one of the major reasons why this kind of line is taken: given the utterly murky nature of the complaint, endless grants to fund endless conferences on the subject await the happy proponent of multiculturalism. But once we return to sober reality, we will accept the obvious impossibility of fulfilling any such program as reason to reject it, even if there were no other.

But of course there are others. In my more modest depiction, our job as teachers in liberal arts programs gives us reason to produce some acquaintance with other cultures—especially a realization that there *are* others; and, very roughly, so far as we know it, some idea of the range of variation there is. But that's the sort of thing to be done, rather than pursuing the impossible idea of total immersion on an equal-exposure basis. And those wishing to do more can go into cultural anthropology, which makes a specialty of the study of cultural diversity. To treat that as a specialty, one among many others, is precisely the right approach, because that is just what it must be, when we consider the matter seriously. For the rest of us, though, to know that there is a vast subject matter out there, and that culture has enormous influence, and something of a few well-chosen examples, must suffice for a liberal education.

What reasons could be advanced for the impossible idea we are tentatively attributing to the advocate of political correctness? There would seem to be two possibilities, in the light of our opening reflections. It could be maintained, say, that all cultures are "equal," e.g., equally "valid" or equally "legitimate," and that this gives each of them a *right* to our attention. Alternatively, it might be claimed that all cultures are equally *good*, equally worthy of study, equally valuable. There is a very large difference between these two—enough, in fact, to make all the difference.

With regard to the first, our response should be simply to agree: cultures are facts, they are comprised of real people, and of course they have a right to exist. But a right to exist is interpretable in two very different ways. The liberal interpretation makes it what is now called a *negative* right, that is, a right that others *not kill or destroy* the persons in question. Illiberal views, on the other hand, will make this a *positive* right: a right that others do something to maintain the rightholders in being, and do it at their own expense into the bargain.

What all of us agree about is the negative version. We are against genocide, aggressive war, murder, and so on. But we do not accept a responsibility to be mother and father, or even aunt and uncle, to every person on the globe. We do not, in particular, owe all these people the duty to bone up on their literatures. Even if it weren't impossible, there would simply be *no reason why we should do so.*

Advocates of political correctness have a few additional problems here, as well. Most cultures have features that are severely frowned upon by those very same advocates when they address specific aspects of our own culture. If they think our culture is male-dominated, they're in for a shock when they look at most others: our own is vastly more liberal than almost all of them. The native tribe in Canada which calls for the removal of one finger per expired husband from widows will serve as an example. If we wish to say that there is *some* sense in which the total culture of which that is one minor aspect is "just as legitimate" as Western culture, fine: they all have the right to be what they are, maybe. But is it being proposed that we really ought to try it ourselves? (In fact, most would, I am sure, scramble to force our own less draconian practices on such people if they could do so.)

Now consider the second charge. As soon as we get into values, of course, we have the very large question of in just what *respect* we are doing the evaluating. There is no end of contexts in which we can make value comparisons, and it must be obvious, on reflection, that there will be things that people in other cultures do which we in ours either cannot or would not dream of trying, or would fail miserably if we did try. When it comes to Roman wrestling, for instance, my plea is a flat "nolo contendre." Some native witch doctors are no doubt much better than any of us at practicing female circumcision with bamboo implements. Should we beat our own breasts about this deficiency?

But presumably when we are talking of such things as core curricula for liberal arts programs, we have in mind the production of bodies of literature—poetry, stories, philosophy, history. Very well: is it seriously maintained that the production of *those kinds* of works, even by all other cultures put together, are equal to those of the Europeans, Americans, or British?

Not in quantity, obviously: European literature dwarfs the rest. Presumably, then, a *qualitative* claim must be intended. But here one scratches one's head. How does one compare the merits of a mid-20th century British novel with a Mayan court edict? If every culture had its *Tom Jones*, we could perhaps make interesting comparisons. But when there isn't anything remotely like it, how is a comparison to proceed? To do that, as I pointed out in the preceding section, one needs common criteria and then one would also need applicable standards. Absent either of these, what is there to do? But one thing is clear enough: if the multiculturalist agenda holds that all cultural products are equally valuable, then in the absence of commensurability, the claim is devoid of sense.

A word should be said here about the philosophical view known as "cultural relativism." This has primarily been considered in the context of moral theory, in which context it has had much interesting discussion and come in for some very heavy weather. One might suppose that it would be more at home in the context of aesthetic theory. But even there, it has its problems. Notable among them is the quite startling popularity in some cultures of artefacts from others. In Canada, Inuit and other native arts have enjoyed a bull market for decades; European classical music is fully as popular in Japan as in England or Germany. Why is this? However you slice it, you're going to have to fix up your favorite version of the theory to accommodate the facts. It won't be easy.

Once you've done that, another problem looms. The claim that all cultures are equal, if it is to be meaningful as a value claim, absolutely requires that there are applicable standards *across* cultures. If all evaluation is locked into a given culture, then any multiculturalist thesis of the sort being contemplated is simply a non-starter. The complete answer to its proposer is, "Look, according to your own theory, the only evaluations I *can* make are ones from the point of view of my own culture. Therefore, your claim that I am doing an injustice to other cultures by not rating them equally with my own is one I can just reject out of hand: In fact, the claim that they are is absolutely meaningless, if you are right." To be sure, that theorist is not right.[3] But that doesn't help either. For once we admit that cultural relativism is not the end of this matter, the advocate must now get down to business and supply genuine, plausible standards of evaluation, such that (1) they are clearly the right ones for the purpose and (2) by those measures, Shakespeare is in truth only equal to the shamanist over in the next village, neither more nor less. Once we did get such criteria—if we ever could—the equality thesis would become totally implausible. Some English novels are far better than others: why shouldn't the same be true of other cultural products?

When the above points have been appreciated, there is simply nothing left of the argument for multiculturalism at the conceptual level. It requires a very high-powered, general theory to support it: somehow, the predominance of Western culture in Western liberal arts curricula is allegedly guilty of "bias" *across the board*. Proponents need to put up or shut up. My perception is that thus far they have done neither.

It is to be expected that evaluation of a given work of literature is going to proceed on the basis of ideas shaped in the culture of the reader. The avid student may well acquire, to some extent, the perceptions of people in alien cultures, and become more or less able to apply criteria operative in those cultures; but such persons are very atypical, and one supposes that literally native adeptness is likely to be beyond their grasp. In some general sense, we may agree, standards for most appraisals are inevitably going to be more or less specific and peculiar to "our" culture—though where "our" is only "European," we are already probably covering far more ground than the case comfortably admits of. Still, we have a phenomenon here, a fact about any recognizable literary world. So the question is, what does it prove regarding the challenge of the multiculturalist?

The first answer is easy, and has already been set out: how could the proponent of political correctness who bases his critique on relativity possibly object to our using standards peculiar to our culture? On such a view, that's exactly what we must inevitably do. Secondly, standards apply to what they apply to, not to other things. It is scarcely possible to apply the sort of standards that might be used in appraising a modern novel to the extremely different literary emanations (if any such can be identified) of some very exotic tribe. This suggests that if our tribesman wants to get "into" European literature, then he's got quite a job ahead of him, just as, if we are to attempt serious value judgments about that culture's special expressions, then we are going to have to find out quite a lot about that culture. This should surprise no one. But it puts politicized programs of multiculturalism in perspective.

Immersing oneself in other cultures is a rather specialized thing to do, and it may or may not strike us as worth doing. There are, after all, perfectly good reasons why one might think it not worth the trouble: I'm not into weight-lifting, nor am I into ancient Chinese poetry. Why do I *have* to be? That is intended to make a point: that parochialism is, in general, quite reasonable. Of course, a *very* parochial reply won't do when we are selecting a liberal arts curriculum. Even so, in speaking to a classroom full of students in a modern university, we are inevitably being to a substantial degree parochial. All of these students, as well as ourselves, will have emerged from some fairly narrow upbringing. We cannot randomize over Ontario, Kamchatka, and Zululand: we will, and should, lose our audience if we do so. The idea of a liberal education is not to replace the typical student with an intellectual Citizen of the World, from everywhere and nowhere. There are plenty of things in this world to study, far too many for any one person to immerse herself in. The ideal of a liberal education makes sense, and is achievable, only if one may, in innumerable cases, note and pass on. In doing so, we come *from* somewhere, and must remain visitors to many of the places we discover in the process of exploration. We can and should achieve breadth and depth; but any idea of *utter* impartiality as between one culture's products and another's is out of any reasonable question.

Even if devoting equal time to all cultures were not an absurd project, one's own culture may reasonably be given pride of place. To know is to plug into Reality—the world we actually live in and deal with. And it is necessarily seen from a particular point of view—one's own. Knowledge of alien cultures can be important and interesting, but there simply is no sense to the idea that they are equally important with one's own, either by any intelligible standard of evaluation or in terms of the fundamental motivation for education in the first place. A sensible reason for devoting most of our attention to our own European (''Western'') heritage is simply that we are immersed in it and are ourselves participants in it. The case for looking into others is fundamentally different.

There are three reasons for studying, in any depth, cultures significantly different from one's own. First, they may well have something to offer. At the conference where an earlier version of some of these remarks was delivered, we were treated to a performance by a traditional Japanese drumming ensemble[4]—material remote from anything Westerners are likely to have encountered, but done with a grace and energy that won over the Western audience instantly and totally. No better argument could be found for including exposure to such things in a program of liberal education. If we set forth to survey great human-istic productions, then those from peoples far away or long ago—or right next door, but hitherto ignored—are tentatively eligible for inclu-sion. But any course necessarily leaves out much that is great and good, for sheer lack of time. We can't do everything in a lifetime, and we can't read everything in one course.

A second good reason could stem from the presence of persons of differing cultures in one's midst, with whom one must deal, and whom therefore it is both prudent and wise to try to understand, sympatheti-cally and in some depth. But it should also be appreciated that in the interplay between smallish cultural groups and the larger surrounding society, the direction of change is inevitably, and reasonably, toward general cultural assimilation by the former outsiders. If I move to Ru-mania, it would be irrational for me to insist on those around me learn-ing English, whereas my learning Rumanian would be a priority. I have no right that the rest of the community bend over backward to learn my language and ways. I will reasonably change a lot in their direction, and they a little in mine. (If I don't like it that way, why didn't I stay home?) Thomas Hobbes proposes as a Law of Nature one he calls "compleas-ance"—that "every man strive to accommodate himself to the rest."[5] He has it just right. Getting on with one's fellows requires give and take, and the ratio of one to the other depends on many things: sheer numbers, who was there first, who has done the most for whom, and so on. But a general willingness to accommodate, rather than to pound on tables, make demands, and erect barricades in the streets, has to be high on any reasonable list.

Finally, there is the potential for better coming to understand one's own milieu, by contrasting it with others that are very different. Getting "into" a very different culture can give one a perspective on one's native culture that could hardly be had otherwise, and one might learn a thing or two that can be adopted in the process. But this too falls very far short of making an acquaintance with all others, equal to that with one's own, a compulsory part of one's curriculum, let alone of one's life.

None of these reasons, then, supports the incoherent idea that all cul-tures are equally deserving of our attention; but they do provide good reason for including some exposure to them on the educational agenda of the seeker after general knowledge.

I take it to be part of the multiculturalist critique that the first part of my program, and perhaps the second, are in severe jeopardy when we broaden our gaze to the reality of ways of thinking very different from our own. To this, it seems to me, there are two promising replies, both reinforced and put in perspective by an observation about the character of any such critique. The observation is this: no such critique could make any sense, to us or anyone, were it not capable of being articulated in a form rendering it communicable and discussable. But as soon as that is admitted, the idea that those very forms themselves are called into question by that critique has around three strikes against it from the start. If what you are trying to say to me, in criticism of my ideas, is, in the light of that very criticism, absolutely unintelligible to me, then why are you bothering to say it? As Tom Lehrer put it, if one's claim is that we cannot communicate, then the very least one can do is to shut up about it! But this is not what our modern multiculturalists do. Instead, they hold large conferences, fill the pages of journals, and generally act as though they really have a genuine message, comparable to the other messages in their respective fields. That is an odd way to run a revolution.

The proposed standard is also applied in singularly skewed fashion. Does one ever hear a supporter of political correctness berating the Malagasi for failing to read Shakespeare? The claim that *we* have this duty although none of the other folks do sounds like a new version of the "white man's burden." The truth is that no one literally owes it to all other cultures to understand them, master their languages, and so on—neither they nor we. Those are no doubt good things to do, and if we cannot do them ourselves we may be happy that someone else does. But *obligation* simply doesn't enter into it.

Suppose, now, that there is a broad program entitled "Classics of Western Civilization." Is it relevant to complain that this leaves out Eastern civilization? The short answer is: of course not. The possibility of offering the other as well may be considered; it will depend on demand by students and capacity to supply with available resources. For that matter, what about Western Barbarism? Why concentrate myopically on "civilization"? In both cases, the reply can be that that just isn't what we're doing. That budgets should be stretched in either direction in the supposed interest of equity is absurd.

All of this, of course, does bring up the vexed question of the status of judgments of intrinsic value. Someone can always be found to pound on the table and insist that Erskine Caldwell is just as valuable as Shakespeare, or that the Iron Butterfly's music is equal to Beethoven's. What is to be said in reply? In part, it will be that when purporting to give a course in subject X, there may be historical criteria applicable. Subject X may be such that author K is a central figure, whatever one may think of K, or for that matter of X. Judgments of intrinsic value are often not the whole show, and perhaps not very much of it. Still, they are fundamental. If X is worth teaching, it must, in the end, be because something in it is of intrinsic interest. One would then have to look at Shakespeare and Erskine Caldwell with suitable care and, insofar as comparison is possible, compare them. The last test has to be the experience of the intelligent and interested person, and if we do not reach agreement at that level, what is there to do but hope that perhaps someday a more acute perception will resolve the matter? Meanwhile, a particular academic institution will just have to affirm its own perceptions and see how it goes.

John Stuart Mill, notoriously, proposed that the preferences of the learned are to be taken as decisive in assessing qualities of pleasure, and he had just such cases in mind.[6] His thesis can hardly be accepted across the board: the person acquainted with both may nevertheless err, and the person acquainted only with one side might, for all that, be acquainted with the right side. But these latter points show us only that the Mill thesis must be taken as a sort of presumption only. The one who doesn't know anything about alternatives is in a weak position to maintain that his own candidates are *better*. Judgments of intrinsic value require experience, and if they are comparative, then experience of both terms of the comparison. In a university, teachers are presumed to be among the learned; insofar as they are not, honesty compels them to own up to their limitations.

Among those limitations will certainly be their level of acquaintance, at least at any great depth, with the works of diverse remote cultures. Most of us in university teaching are simply not in a position to say on the basis of scholarly experience that there have been no Shakespeares of the twenty-second century B.C. We must rely on the word of those who know more than we. Even so, our case is likely to be better than those whose sole reason for insisting that we add some hitherto unknown item to our list of "classics" is that All Literature is Equal, or something of the sort. *A priori* premises about the value of all humans or all cultures or all whatevers are certain to be at the root of such complaints, and if so, the complaints are baseless. These just are not *a priori* matters. The proof of artistic puddings has to be in the eating, and those who have not even tasted are not worth listening to. And those who have, but who insist on first etherizing their taste buds with a large helping of ideology, so that they can't distinguish anything from anything, are no better—actually, they are worse, for instead of offering us nothing, they offer us fraudulent "goods": they make claims requiring real experience when instead what they have is the "experience" of an ideological trance. You can't hear if you don't listen, and if you haven't heard, then you can't judge a string quartet, any more than you can evaluate a treatise in econometrics.

Reasons supporting multiculturalism, then, fall far short of what would be needed for the sort of revolution proposed. An interest in diversity for its own sake, for its instructive value, and as an accommodation to the presence of others in our midst, prompts attention to humanistic works from other cultures. But nothing argues coherently for, and very much argues against, the proposal to elevate the products of all other cultures to equal status in a curriculum.

Deconstruction

The next item on our list is the question of "whether concepts such as truth, objectivity, and impartiality can have any real application in view of the challenges of deconstruction and its neighbors." As my opening remarks about general politicization suggest, I have scant sympathy for the supposed challenges in question. This is not because there are no problems about truth, objectivity, and impartiality, but because no "challenge" of the type and at the level supposedly offered by deconstruction has the remotest prospect of impugning them in a meaningful manner, or of supplying support for any political or moral programs, of political correctness or any other.

The thesis is supposed to be that there is a problem about the *concept* of truth, a problem of the kind that casts doubt on its employability *tout court*. This is puzzling. There are problems about some concepts, or perhaps we should say putative concepts: the concept of a round square, for example, is such that we can see, upon reflection, that there is no question of there actually *being* any of those things, since whatever would qualify an item for the characterization "square" would on that account disqualify it for the description "round." But does deconstruction say anything like that about truth? Truth is the relation holding between a statement and the world when the world is the way the statement says it is. To say that is, of course, to assume that we can distinguish between statement and world. But while philosophers have alleged that doubt can be cast on this, one has to wonder what they think they are talking about when they say so, since it is a distinction any child can appreciate, in a vast array of typical cases. The child hears someone uttering a bunch of noises, and ere long comes to discern which of them are statements and which not; when she learns to read, she in turn learns to correlate marks on paper with those noises, and so on. She has no great difficulty in telling that there are things in the area that have the function of *saying* something, as distinct from other things that do not; and that when something is said, what is said is often *about* some of the other things. Notice that the recipient of a statement is going to have to be able to identify objects and situations in the world in order to have the concept of a statement *at all*: the things we are talking about crop up, as I put it, in the speaker's environment, along with all sorts of other things. And these other things, as she also soon learns, are available for description, querying, and so on, by means of the deployed sentences and their equivalents. As to which items in the nonlinguistic environment to be on the lookout for, given certain items from the linguistic one, that too is not perceived as *fundamentally* problematic. For if the child, or any of us, understands the component concepts in the sentence in question, we thereby know where to look; or, in some cases, we are puzzled and then, if we are curious or have a practical interest in the matter, we shop around for clarification and explanation. In the innumerable relatively puzzle-free cases, we know what it would be for a sentence to be true or false, and in a sizable subset of those, we even know *whether* it is. I glance out the window, and discern that we are not in the midst of a snowstorm. Deconstructionists insist that I must have a ''motive'' in this. And indeed I did— two, in fact. First, I wanted a good example of a sentence whose truth conditions are relatively straightforward and of whose truth I am in fact aware. The other is that I'm considering going out and want to know how to dress. Both are familiar, neither are philosophically puzzling.

There is plenty for us humans to be philosophically puzzled about: numbers, microphysical entities, the being of concepts or ideas themselves, and so on through the philosophical repertoire; where the saltshaker could have disappeared to since dinner is at the opposite end of the spectrum, but still puzzling. But the deconstructionist's arguments aren't pitched at either of those levels. If they worked at all, they would have to work at the *ordinary* level. Talk of blizzards, crockery, sparrows, you name it: all would be suspect, in fact so utterly up in the air that we should have to abandon language altogether. Regarding such so-called theories we cannot, I think, improve on John Searle's thesis:

> I am not claiming that one can prove metaphysical realism to be true from some standpoint that exists apart from our human linguistic practices. What I am arguing, rather, is that those practices themselves presuppose

metaphysical realism. So one cannot within those practices intelligibly deny metaphysical realism, because the meaningfulness of our public utterances already presupposes an independently existing reality to which expressions in those utterances can refer. Metaphysical realism is thus not a thesis or a theory; it is rather the condition of having theses or theories or even of denying theses or theories.[7]

It would be fun to put these observations in a more highfalutin style, no doubt. But it is sufficient to say that Derrida and the others could only have a genuine argument if it preserved enough sense to leave language usable and therefore intelligible. Yet as soon as it does that, it is bereft of a thesis general enough to have any interesting effect on present controversies. That all theses about anything are indeed theses, and thus expressed in some language or other, is an obvious truth; but that we are therefore incapable of deciding in a manner free of bias whether any particular word does or does not refer to any particular thing is so far the reverse of the truth that if it were true, nobody would be able to recognize or express the alleged "fact."

In his relatively clear-headed exposition of Derridian deconstruction, Stephen White begins by characterizing the linguistic work of Ferdinand de Saussure thus:

> Rather than trying to understand meaning according to the traditional model by analyzing the relationship of words to their referents (i.e., things in the world), Saussure began to tie meaning more to the relationship of signs . . . to one another. It is from the differences between signs in a system of signs that the meaning of any given sign arises.[8]

White uses the comparative term "more," to be sure. But he also uses the rather precise expression "rather than," thus implying that the allegedly new way of understanding language actually rejected the idea that words have anything to do with reality, ever actually refer to anything. The reader should think about that for a moment. Is it, in truth, conceivable at all—does it make any sense whatever—to suppose that words do have meaning, and yet have it *entirely* by their relations to *other words*? If the answer isn't obvious, you might start by asking how you knew that the things you just read were, in fact, words rather than, say, gyroscopes, spiral nebulae, apartment houses, or rainstorms. And why in the case of each of the latter, reasonably clear images of certain *things* (namely gyroscopes, spiral nebulae, apartment houses, or rainstorms) come to mind as being what these words are about, rather than images merely of *more words,* or for that matter of random other objects. Or how we are to locate and identify any of these things out there that we call "words"—since, obviously, words are also, while they're at it, things—sounds, marks on blackboards, and so on. And finally, why the theorist should be so loathe to grant reality to all the *other* things in the world if he grants it to words. And so on . . .

Here's an illustration of the supposed method in practice. White goes on to mention a supposed criticism of an important political theory, Hobbes's, by Michael Ryan, said to be a

> deconstruction of Hobbes's foundational opposition between reason and the clear uses of language, on the one hand, and unreason and the ambiguous and metaphorical use of language, on the other. The first half of the opposition delimits the sphere of what is privileged and foundational for the construction of a secure political world; the second half, the sphere of what is marginal, suspicious, and ultimately seditious—what post-structuralists often refer to as the "Other."

White then says that "Ryan deconstructs Hobbes's imposing edifice by pointing out that it undermines its own authority by appealing at the start to the metaphor of a leviathan."[9]

Are we supposed to be impressed by this? Apparently Ryan thinks that in using a metaphorical name for a book whose theory is intended to be anything but, Hobbes is somehow undermining his own thesis. Well, *how*? Readers know what Hobbes intends by this term, and the idea that somehow the edifice itself is subjected to a damaging criticism by being published under a title conveying a metaphor is delivered up as if it were a remarkable and unsettling discovery, instead of the trivial fact it is. Evidently, if we are to follow White's thesis, had Hobbes named it something else, say "The Rational Principles of Politics," he would have been back in business! Well, if one can't distinguish words from the world in the first place, it is easy enough to see how someone might persuade himself that the so-called "deconstruction" in question is indeed a *deconstruction*, a criticism that goes to the heart of what is allegedly deconstructed, destroying its claims to his credence. The rest of us, though, will manage to get on well enough. And in this case, the theorist will have disavailed himself of the pleasure and instruction of reading the most challenging of all political theorists.

Consider Professor White's summary of the position of one camp of postmodernists as against another: "Caricaturing slightly: All contexts are fictions, but the ones in which we find ourselves embedded have a special legitimacy."[10] Did he say "slightly"? Anyone who could liter-

ally *believe* the first part would, of course, be at a loss to account for
the meaning of the rest: if *all* contexts are fictitious, then there is *no
sense* to the idea that *one* of those is "the one that we are embedded
in." But then, anyone who could believe anything of the sort has long
since departed for Cloud Cuckooland anyway: why should such a person bother to pick nits about which mythical "context" for somebody
called "we" (Who? Which novel's cast of characters, and picked on
what basis?) to do what used to be real political and social philosophy,
or science, or anything else? For the rest of us, who can generally tell
words from what they're about, this will strike us as a silly game, and
no more. The point about literal description, as in history, say, is precisely that it is *not* fiction, and is thus amenable to standards of evidence
that fiction is not.

But what about "impartiality" and "objectivity," then? Again, the
point is that no amount of deconstruction is in principle capable of
convicting all use of language of being prone to critically significant
defects on the score of either. When we find that some people, to our
surprise, are color-blind or tone deaf, the point is brought home to us
that to perceive the world we must have perceptual apparatus, and that
this apparatus can vary. If this impugned the whole idea of objectivity,
we would be in a bad way. But it doesn't. The colorblind know that
others see color-distinctions where they see none, and more generally,
we can develop criteria that correct for subjective variance. We can
make corrections of inaccurate estimates, due to over-hasty application
of the apparatus as well as to inadequacies inherent in it. We could
not, however, make any such corrections on the basis of a supposed
philosophical claim that the quantity we are trying to measure is just a
figment of speech anyway: for in every reasonable sense of those words,
it is *not* a figment. When deconstructionists get into their cars and drive
off, they do not, if they have any sense, let their doubts about the objective reference of such terms as "car" and "gearshift" get in the way
of their tendency to keep right, shift up when needed, and the rest of it.
But it is just that kind of thing—real-world stuff—that is at issue in
the political correctness controversies. The classical social philosophers
knew better, and so should modern readers. It goes without saying that
these trendy postmodernist fancies do nothing at all to support any program of political action, be it the politically correct ones or any other.
They are in precisely the same theoretical boat as the several other
examples discussed above.

This way with what has been a mightily influential "critical" theory
in recent thought has, certainly, been short, and some readers will find

that ground for suspicion. They might bear in mind that Derrida's own way with the likes of Descartes is even shorter. Deconstructionism is one of those many fads that promise to make philosophy really easy instead of the hard intellectual labor it actually is. Since according to deconstructionism's view of the matter, no theory about anything is actually about anything outside of itself, so-called deconstructionist criticism becomes as easy as knocking down a house of cards. After all, if you can't tell a card from anything else, why not play such games? What else, indeed, would there be to do?

Political Correctness on the Job Front: Affirmative Action

We now come to what has probably become the practically most important of our questions, the one to which "affirmative action" has been the politically correct response. Does justice require that hitherto persecuted or oppressed or anyway nonprivileged groups be given preference in hiring? I focus especially on academic hiring, though the idea applies also in the context of bestowing assorted academic rewards or distinctions, and of course in hiring in any other area of work.

Often I will speak not only of "oppressed" groups, but of *allegedly* oppressed ones, for the question of just what constitutes oppression is a major one in the contemporary world. Slaves, for example, were, I take it as obvious, oppressed; but there is room for doubt that contemporary American women, as a class, are so. My discussion will largely concentrate on the question of whether affirmative action would be a reasonable program even if the claimed history of oppression for the intended beneficiaries is true. But the ways of political correctness not only distort the remedy, as I shall argue, but they also greatly distort the supposed situation to be remedied. This cannot be left entirely out of consideration.

People are hired in order to perform fairly well-defined tasks, and in most cases, what constitutes good performance at those tasks is fairly clear. But sometimes not: What matters may be elusive qualities requiring the discernment of experience and the intuition of the entrepreneur, the manager, or, say, the academic "superior" to spot, without the help of formalized specification. Moreover, it is assumed that those doing the hiring have a real interest in performance, especially to performance given a constrainingly finite budget: those hiring normally want to get the best performance for the least expenditure, be that expenditure monetarily or otherwise defined. When the circumstances are greatly different from those, the question takes on a very different meaning, or could lose meaning altogether. The Deity, possessed of an infinite budget, would be hard-put to argue that He/She cannot afford to place so-and-so among the Elect; but hard-pressed managers, directors, and department chairpersons can and must. However, affirmative action forces the manager or administrator to make decisions that are, given the interests of the firm (or the academy) *uneconomic*. Applicant A asks the same salary as Applicant B and is evidently able to do the job more effectively; yet our administrator is told that she *must* hire B, whether she likes it or not. And this, she is told, is because *justice requires it.*

It is of crucial importance that that is the claim. She is not told that she must hire B on the ground, say, that B is the nephew of the owner of the firm. From the manager's point of view, that would be an irrelevancy, a nuisance, or in some cases a disaster—but at least it's not claimed that justice has anything to do with it. But everybody argues for politically correct hiring on that ground: justice, fairness, equity are the watchwords. But fairness or equity cannot function independently here. If they are not advanced under the banner of justice, they cannot be advanced at all. If justice does not require fairness, then the fact that one was not thus fair is no ground for the kind of coercive intervention that affirmative action consists in.

The subject of justice, of course, has long been a preoccupation of philosophers, who since Plato have advanced articulate theories on the matter. Plato also thought that in the ideal republic, philosophers would be kings—a suggestion that has not met with a uniformly favorable reception by subsequent philosophers. In Plato's case, those philosophers would be made kings on the ground that they *knew what was good for people*—and knew it better than those people themselves. Over the course of two thousand years, the thought that perhaps this isn't such a good idea, that maybe we should instead be letting people decide for themselves what is good or bad for them, began to make its way to the forefront of philosophical consciousness. That basic idea, I think, continues to be the only plausible one in the field. But it is easily misunderstood. Indeed, as I have been arguing, political correctness is due to just such a misunderstanding. But in no case is this misunderstanding clearer or more devastating in its consequences than in the context of hiring. I will suggest, in fact, that affirmative action is exactly what you would expect from ''philosopher kings''—philosophers in the grip of a fallacious theory but put in power, or rather, philosophers formulating such a theory and then letting it slip out of the Academy, where it would only be discussed by fellow ivory-tower types, out into the halls of Parliament and onto the political hustings, where the damage it can do is essentially unlimited.

Affirmative action intervenes in the actions of individuals or associations, and intervenes in ways that are contrary to the interests and values of those individuals and associations. To do this is prima facie wrong: *private* actions of that kind ("Hire my brother, or I'll shoot!") would rightly be regarded as criminal. This fact about affirmative action is often obscured, and it is easy enough, as we shall see, to understand why it is so. But it needs to be kept in the limelight. The issue before us is *not* whether it is merely *okay* for people to hire on the basis of such odd factors as race or gender, but whether it is okay for public agencies to *force* them to hire on such bases. This has been so widely misunderstood as to obscure the question almost hopelessly. We must try to put things right.

Those who defend programs of affirmative action do have a picture to paint, a somewhat articulate account of their rationales that we may count as a "theory," indeed. But they tend to paint a picture differing in a crucial way from what I claimed above. For they tend to attribute to the hirers an anti-economic motivation of just the kind that I centrally ascribe to the program of affirmative action itself. The political correctness claim on behalf of affirmative action is that managers survey employees and, noting that those employees are of the putatively unwanted race, sex, religion, or whatever, reject those applicants *regardless* of their expected contribution to the profitability or otherwise-measured success of the enterprise in question. In fact, the theory of affirmative action requires the attribution of motives to hirers that are quite analogous to those ascribed to witches in the 14th century: they are possessed of evil spirits, driving them to do wicked things.

It is intriguing how deeply ingrained among affirmative action proponents is this syndrome. Yet on the face of it, it is incoherent. Consider first the paradigmatic case of hiring in a firm devoted solely to profit. Somehow, affirmative action supposes, we are to understand that such people will turn down a person of the "wrong" sex, color, or whatever, despite this person's probable greater contribution to the profitableness of the entrepreneur's firm. How could this be? No doubt business people are not conspicuously more rational than the rest of us, but it is surely quite another matter to suppose that they are inherently far less so. Why would they deviate in this way from their central aim—to make money?

Now, one way to get the political correctness argument off the ground would be by misunderstanding the purpose of the selected association. The proponent of affirmative action will note, for instance, that the business entrepreneur might, in some circumstances, be disposed to pay less to persons in the oppressed class than they would to some others for what they agree is similar work: women, say, or black people, than persons in the allegedly oppressing class, say white males, for the same work. For of course they would—just as they would hire a white applicant who would do the job for less than another white applicant, and just as an entrepreneur of any race or sex would. The rational profit-seeker makes the best bargain possible, and if some large class of people is available cheaper but will do the job just as well, they will of course get the nod.

It is quite true that the entrepreneur is largely indifferent to the reasons why a given applicant would settle for less. Perhaps that applicant is desperate, or really doesn't want to move to Seattle, or doesn't need the money so much but simply wants to have something to do. No matter. From the entrepreneur's narrow point of view, the best candidate is the one who maximizes profits for the firm. That is the entrepreneur's criterion of efficiency, and not, for example, "equal pay for equal work," taken as a goal in its own right. The entrepreneur, to be sure, does end up paying equally for equal work, provided that we understand "equal work" to mean work of equal marginal profitability, and that the equality of pay is simply due to the operation of this motive, rather than an independent motive in its own right. Too many enthusiasts for legislation on these matters, however, have assumed that these other goals are what business people are supposed to be aiming at. But why should they?

You don't buy all the boxes of Wheaties on the shelf on the ground that they all cost the same, or refuse to buy at a lower price on the ground that that price differs from someone else's price for the same thing. Instead, you account yourself fortunate to have got a bargain, and move on to the next project with a bit more in pocket than you would otherwise have had. Only people who are spending other people's money, without their consent—mainly persons in positions of political power—profess to be motivated by equality as an objective distinct from the purposes, educational or commercial or whatever, that the organization exists to promote.

In a free market, everything is done by mutual agreement. A makes an offer on the basis of perceived interest to A, B considers it on the basis of perceived interest to B, and accepts or declines it as B's own judgment dictates. Given such a system, we can understand notions of efficiency: it is what maximizes achievement of the goals of the person concerned. They do what they do because they are *interested* in it. Under the circumstances, the idea that the managerial or entrepreneurial actors on the scene have an interest in expensive things like racial discrimination, an interest needing to be "corrected" by the rulers, doesn't make any general sense. Insofar as a manager or an entrepreneur genuinely discriminates, that entrepreneur acts irrationally.

That associations are often run on bases other than (monetary) profit is true and important. Churches, for example, are not: they discriminate against the heathen, including in their hiring practices, which of course discriminate on the basis of religion. Except, of course, that in their case, or at least from their point of view, it *isn't* "discrimination": they are not hiring on grounds irrelevant or contrary to their central purposes, but in fact central to them. Similarly, modelling agencies "discriminate" against the fat, the shapeless, and so on. As of course they should. In general, hirers discriminate against the less competent. Only that is not usually called "discrimination."

Now it may well be that a firm operates in an environment permeated by racism, sexism, or whatever, and that in consequence he cannot operate in the otherwise maximally profitable way. When the Brooklyn Dodgers broke the color barriers in the National Baseball League by hiring the brilliant black player Jackie Robinson, they did so upon a judgment that fans were more interested in baseball than in color, though they faced many problems posed by access to hotels and the like, many of which would not accept a black person, despite evident capability and willingness to pay the going rate. In the case of the hotels, they judged that if they accepted black patrons, they would lose business among white patrons, whom they supposed to be racist. But one hotel catering to both races is more efficient than two catering only to one each, just as one top-level league hiring the best players provides entertainment for fans that they are likely to prefer, being fans, to the sort they can get by restricting themselves to players of their own race. A National League team that tried to play with exclusively white players would be digging its own economic grave. We know in hindsight that the Dodgers' business decision was a major success in economic terms. Rational economic decision-making here strongly pointed toward breaking the existing color barriers, which were imposed by forces *outside* the firm, not by the forces of profit as such. Profit is color-blind, even if people often aren't.

A similar claim among political correctness advocates of affirmative action today is that, say, women, if hired at all, would be hired at wages

below the fair level. The reply is the same. It is not the fault of the firm
in question if exogenous factors have made that group available at bargain prices. As a rational firm, their response to this would be to jump
at the opportunity thus provided, just as firms able to utilize less costly
third-world labor effectively will do so by setting up foreign plants, and
just as countless American enterprises did when legal and social barriers to interracial hiring were lifted. Again, the point is that economic
reason does not create, nor does it reinforce such discrimination, if it
exists, because discrimination, as normally defined, is unprofitable;
rather, it tends to eradicate them.

And in fact, it has done so. The belief in disparities of pay between
males and females in business contexts today are largely—perhaps entirely—by-products of bad statistical reasoning, not the real facts of
life. For example, the widely quoted alleged disparity of some thirty
per cent between men's and women's average pay fails to distinguish
full-time and part-time employment. Further sources of disparity suc-
cumb to closer investigation as well: the facts that adult women have
children, keeping them away from work for some time, or are less likely
to be permanent, more likely to take frequent leave, and for various
other reasons tend to entail higher employee costs than males, all explain why women as a group would earn less than men. Once all those
factors are taken into account, disparities disappear.[11] There is, in fact,
no "correcting" to be done by affirmative action programs.

There is no argument for affirmative action, in short, on the grounds
originally alleged. In the ordinary sense of the term "discrimination,"
people acting in their own economic interest do not discriminate. But
in fact, the argument tends subtly to change color. For now it is claimed
that employers owe females more than males, or blacks more than
whites. This is usually obscured by the tendency to insist that what they
are claiming is that they owe them "the same." But if one looks at the
fine print, one suddenly sees that it is not the "same" in the sense that
matters: namely, equal expenditure by the employer. Rather, the call is
for employers to pay the same, say, per hour, and then in addition,
without any compensation to the employer, to pay also the extra expense entailed by maternity leave or any number of other factors. Thus
it is claimed that employers owe women day-care facilities and other
amenities not formerly included in wages—owe it to them in addition
to their paycheques. Or professors owe indifferent black students higher
grades than they would award to equally indifferent white ones. The
higher costs of hiring females, or giving grades to black students, are
now alleged to be a social duty of employers or teachers, a new duty of

justice! Justice, it seems, requires irrational behavior. I suggest, instead, that a theory that says that is an irrational theory of justice.

The next point to appreciate is that there is no *a priori* reason why we should expect relevant variables of performance in any given area of endeavour to be, without exception, randomly related to the politically incorrect variables. Many proponents seem to hope, may well want to believe, that persons of all sexes, races, and heights must be equally competent, deep down inside—at golf, basketball, hockey, chess, selling insurance, nuclear physics, needlework, teaching philosophy, and so on indefinitely. But we have no business at all forming beliefs on these matters independently of empirical evidence; and the evidence in all sorts of areas disconfirms that belief so resoundingly that we really must dub the belief a *prejudice*. The incidence of outstanding talent at basketball, for example, so far as all empirical evidence is concerned, is not randomly related to those variables. The likelihood that a person with the optimal combination of height, speed, reflexes, and so on, for outstanding success at the game of basketball will turn out to be tall, black, and male is far higher than that the individual will be short, female, white, or yellow. We have no reason at all to think that the presence of so many tall black males on pro basketball teams is either a bizarre accident, or due to rampant discrimination against whites, Asians, females, and midgets. And if you then move to other areas of endeavor, those same ultracompetent basketball players will rarely be found doing fine needlework, or differential equations, or running the corner store. So it goes. Common sense is here abetted by genetic theory, which assures us that individual and group variability, rather than uniformity, is the norm. Given the number of human genes and the principles of random mixing involved, the probability of two persons who aren't genetic twins being identical is astronomically low; and similarly, the probability that all humans are identical in any interesting respect, such as basic intelligence, skill at anything that requires skill, or physique, is nil. On the other hand, the probability that genetically homogeneous groups will differ nonrandomly from other groups in various ''irrelevant'' respects is enormous. Only those with some kind of fixation about human ''equality''—or, of course, a strong political interest in it—will be either surprised or discomfited at this. But such fixations are not a satisfactory basis for imposing coercive restrictions on the hiring behavior of people pursuing perfectly legitimate goals, such as basketball, church work, and teaching philosophy. For this, one ought to have good evidence, not shoddy statistical sophistry or genetic fantasy.

Similarly, there is no reason at all to think that the wages of those same extremely competent basketball players ought in principle to be identical to those of your typical unemployable, or even your typical plumber, despite the far more "essential" nature of the services offered by the latter as compared with the ballplayer. The actions of people with freedom to choose what they will do with their money determine these things, and those actions bring it about that professional basketball is currently an extremely remunerative occupation for those with the required (astronomical) level of talent.

Returning now to the central issue, let me again remind the reader of the essential point: the question is not whether anyone may ever hire anyone for reasons other than certain narrowly defined ones pertaining to performance at specified tasks. Of course they may, and every now and again they have excellent reason to do so. The question is, rather, whether we, the public, may *require* the manager or administrator to hire in ways that fly in the face of her judgments of reasonable performance toward whatever goals the institution she works with may be concerned to pursue, be they educational, commercial, or whatever. The manager's or the entrepreneur's judgments of those matters, we should be well aware, are certain to be better than ours. There is no question of affirmative action or equal-pay legislation being reasonably expected to improve the output of the economy, or of the university, or whatever other undertaking is in question. Prima facie, it's just the opposite: imposing restrictions on the efficient pursuit of legitimate activities is inefficient. When the dean informs department X, which unanimously preferred the highly competent white male to the female who not only lacked the doctorate but doesn't even have the specialty needed by that department, that they must hire her in the name of "equity,"[12] we should not expect educational goals to be effectively forwarded.

If there were any good reason to think otherwise, such intervention wouldn't *be* affirmative action. In an effort to preserve the idea that affirmative action is efficient despite these considerations, the administrations in Canadian universities, as no doubt in American ones, insist that "academic standards are not to be impugned"—hiring committees are only to prefer the female, or the Native Canadian, or whatever, "other things equal"—so long, that is, as the result is that you end up employing roughly x per cent members of those groups, x being a figure often far out of touch with reality so far as relevant demonstrated competence is concerned. But the "other things equal" stricture is insincere. If you genuinely don't know which candidate is better along dimension X, there are plenty of further dimensions, Y, to explore instead;

deciding which is better in ways relevant to the academic aims of the department concerned is almost never impossible. But an affirmative action requirement of the type in question ensures that this process will end very early, by *decreeing* what shall count as "equal." And it will then invariably decide for the preferred group, by overruling any decision against it. "Hire female (or whatever), other things equal!" turns out to be functionally equivalent to "Hire female—or else!"

Here's how it works. First, the hirers traditionally assemble, from the many applications received, a "short list" of candidates for the job. However, in the interests of "equity," of course, this list *must* contain at least some candidates of the politically correct varieties. This object is promoted by the fact that the committee in charge of assembling the short list has itself been required to contain some members of the politically correct groups. Once the short list is assembled, the view is taken that, after all, everyone on the short list must be "equal"— whether there is any real reason to think so or not. And so the "equal-best" always turns out to be from the desired group. Such procedures virtually guarantee that decisions on these matters will not be made in the best academic interests of the institution in question. What were alleged to be considerations of equity have become certain means of inequity.

Justice is thought by many to be an entirely different thing from efficiency, to be sure, and at some level this is of course true. Justice can certainly insist that you choose x over y even if you would much prefer y to x, because y would get you what you want, in the circumstances. Violence, for example, often pays; but even when it does, justice requires that we forego that method of promoting our interests. However, it is a very different matter to say that justice can insist that you choose x over y when the basis of your preference for y is that it better serves a perfectly legitimate undertaking.

But let us, for the sake of argument, suppose that it can. The question now is: should the consideration that the candidate in question is from an oppressed group constitute a reason that can be pressed in the interests of justice on behalf of an otherwise uneconomic and unwise decision? In putting my question this way, I should point out, I am implicitly rejecting a claim that many enthusiasts would want to insist on: namely, that justice requires that we hire the ablest, or most capable, or whatever. There are two reasons to deny this. We have already seen one: You may not be able to afford the best; hiring the best without thought of cost is inefficient. But a more fundamental reason is that we are not constrained by justice, though we are encouraged by economic self-interest, to operate our businesses in the most efficient manner anyway.

In private employment, we *may* hire the less competent, if we insist. It is normally in one's interest to hire the more competent, yes: but then, what if the owners of the enterprise are perfectly happy to make less than economically ideal decisions? In a free society, it is still not right, not, in fact, fair, to force them to act otherwise. Yet that is what affirmative action proposes: we will be required, by force of law, to make decisions in the way the legislators, or whoever, tell us to, rather than as we think best. In the academy, it may not be a matter of law, strictly. But if it is administration policy operating against academic departments, then the situation is analogous, though not identical. The issue, then, is: does society have any right to impose on us in those ways?

What are the arguments for affirmative action? We have seen that it cannot be to aid academic or any other kind of efficiency. The next obvious thought that comes to mind is that the oppressed are owed these preferences as a matter of *compensation*. Of course, if that were so, it would justify imposing on people to effect the appropriate compensation. But this idea completely misses the mark in the case of affirmative action. For affirmative action does *not* reward individuals who have been, in the relevant ways, unjustly treated, assuming even that those "ways" are unjust. Nor does it penalize those who have been responsible for any such unjust treatment. When you prefer an individual on the sheer ground that a *group* of which he or she is a member is or was oppressed, you set aside what must be the only relevant question if it were genuinely a matter of compensation: namely, whether the person we propose to stick with the penalty actually committed the "crime" in question. In the case of affirmative action, the answer is virtually always in the negative. The slaves in the antebellum South of the United States were no doubt owed considerable compensation, but they and their masters are long since gone from the scene and there is no rational way to calculate just compensations for their descendants, nor to determine who among the descendants of the former slave-owners should be forced to pay it. And in the rare case in which a charge of overt discrimination in hiring could be proved, the individual in question would, on the hypothesis on which affirmative action is based, be able to sue for damages in court. But hauling whole groups into court, regardless of their individual relations to the supposed victims, is wildly against any principle of justice here. If the occasional department turned down some applicant because she was female, this hardly justifies us in requiring all departments to hire females in some allotted proportion— any more than if this or that Jewish businessman in pre-Hitler Germany overcharged this or that person on this or that occasion, it does not justify sending six million of them off to the gas chamber for their sins.

It has also been proposed that group oppression of the X's brings it about that the non-X's have been collective beneficiaries of those wrongful acts, in the sense that they are now in a better position to profit from society's opportunities than the X's. Now, such arguments require the assumption that "society's opportunities" are *owed,* in equal measure, to all of its members; the phrase "equal opportunity" is flourished as if it were a self-evidently reasonable goal of society to bring it about. But those who flourish this popular cliché of the day do not realize what they are getting into. Just as was the case with cultures being entitled to "equal time" in liberal educational curricula, so with the present proposal, in any meaningful form: No society, actual or possible, could ever offer meaningful and equal opportunities at everything to everyone, no matter how hard it tried. The goal is strictly nonsensical. The bloke in Vladivostok whose mother failed to teach him how to sew and whose fingers are too stubby and stiff to manipulate a needle anyway does not and cannot have "equal opportunity" to work in a dress-making establishment; and spending massive amounts of time and effort rectifying that supposed inequity is, in addition to being silly and futile, utterly arbitrary. And by being so, it is also unjust, and is so in principle.

There is no way to avoid that result. There are a literally endless number of distinctions of one person from another that can be relevant to someone interested in hiring someone else for some useful purpose; the idea that either the employer or her society lies under a constraint to see to it that for all values of those variables, none should be allowed to have a differential effect on the probability of being hired for each of those indefinitely large number of kinds of positions is obviously beyond anyone's capacity to achieve, even if it were a sane goal in the first place. Hiring is sensitive to differences in specifically relevant capability, and insensitive to the details of how the different candidates came to be different in those respects.

The reason why "politically correct" describes the goal of affirmative action so accurately is that there is no nonarbitrary basis for singling out femaleness or blackness from among the countless dimensions along which people are undoubtedly disproportionately represented in any number of employments, and then requiring employment to match *those* variables and not the others. The short, the left-handed, the Polish, the ones with an odd twitch—as I say, the list is literally endless. But sex and color are easy to spot, so it is easy to assemble them into a political pressure group; and in a democracy, the squeaky wheel will get the grease. The claim, however, that justice uniquely singles out these groups for collective rectification is without rational basis.

To advance the cause of affirmative action under the banner of general equal opportunity, therefore, is to defend the implausible by the unintelligible. Whenever anyone hires anyone for anything the employer picks that person in preference to all who lacked the qualities of the winning candidates, and in so doing undoubtedly alters by a minute amount the percentage in the employment statistics of those in logically unrelated classes who have or don't have the qualities in question. For "society" to insist that the employer in question pay heed to some of those variables and not others is for it to throw its weight behind one group and against another. This preference for the one group against the other is arbitrary, and arbitrary interventions in the activities of people are precisely what the liberal outlook on justice condemns.

Here is where the potential for subtle but far-reachingly significant misunderstanding is perhaps at its greatest. There is nothing inherently wrong with arbitrary choices by individuals. You prefer chocolate to vanilla? Fine! You like this spoon better than that one? Fine! You prefer Charlie to John, despite the latter's superior intelligence and more engaging personality? If I'm John and I like you, that may not be so fine with me—but it's your choice. There is no question of injustice here, whatever you do. But forcing people to choose against their own preferences—however arbitrary those preferences themselves may be—rather than letting them do as they would like, is another matter. Here we cannot be arbitrary. Here arbitrariness *is* injustice, a case of some people exercising coercion over others who have done no harm to anyone.

When the Province of Ontario brought down a major program of legislation establishing what amount to quotas of required hiring of members of certain specific politically in groups, this was described in the news media in such language as "tearing down the last barriers" to advancement on the part of members of those groups. Advertising of that type is typical with such programs, and like its counterpart in the seedier areas of commerce, it is misleading. It is, more precisely, "hype." For there were not, in Ontario's case, any barriers of the kind implied in such descriptions. Nobody in Ontario lay under any compulsion to refuse to hire this, that, or the other sort of person to this, that, or the other sort of enterprise on grounds of such factors as sex or race—not, that is, until affirmative action got into the act. Many do lie under a perfectly intelligible interest to do such things: no males will be hired to model women's underwear, black actors will be preferred for playing Othello, and so on. And beyond question, many of the desired attributes in various endeavours correlate rather strikingly with some of those factors. The National Basketball Association of the United States does not actually discriminate against Asians, Caucasians, or the short, but you will find precious few of them, and inordinate numbers of rangy black men, on those teams. In the absence of any positive duty of justice that one play basketball, or turn all and sundry into basketball players, the case for using force of law to enlist a few midgets, or women of normal dimensions, to play on the Lakers is not just modest but nonexistent.[13]

One could go on indefinitely with such cases. In no occupation is it reasonable to assume, a priori, that qualities making for success in it are necessarily distributed in any particular fashion with respect to sex, color, religion, or any other of the currently popular variables. The idea, therefore, that an employer *must* be "discriminating against" those belonging to some groups said to be "under-represented" in the ranks of those employed by him or her is without basic foundation. Add to this the fact that it is in the interest of an employer to hire the most productive people he or she can, so that what is normally claimed to be discrimination is prima facie irrational in any case, and the whole theory behind the current concern over discrimination and affirmative action is, as they say, blown out of the water.

In the special case of the higher education environment, some further considerations complicate matters. Many colleges and universities are publicly owned and operated, and others are owned and operated by religious organizations. He who pays the piper calls the tune, and when the piper is the government, one might suppose that the educational institution in question must be wholly subservient to the political climate of the day; when it is a religious institution, it may prefer religious purity to academic integrity. May it not?

But we may instead hold that the purpose of educational institutions, whoever sponsors them, is to educate. If they educate on the assumption that some favored doctrine is true, they nevertheless, if they are serious, must be open to contrary evidence; on no other condition do they qualify as educational. If current governments subscribe to ideologies of the day, and these are incompatible with the aims of education as such, then its academic administrators should take the line that the aims of education outweigh those of current governments, and do so because they are more consonant with the most reasonable aims of society. At any rate, I shall take it that the aforementioned complications arising from these differing auspices may be set aside here.

To say that there is "a" purpose of education is no doubt to run a danger of misleading. Education is spreading knowledge—but knowledge of what? Much of my discussion has been concerned with the specific idea of ''liberal'' education; but much education is certainly not liberal in that rather special sense, nor is there anything wrong with that. Nevertheless, there are commonalities about education, no matter what is taught or why. We educate only when we impart knowledge—not, for instance, when we indoctrinate, inculcate, or impart a skill, unless it is one of the many skills useful in acquiring knowledge. And whatever might be said these days among philosophers about the analysis of knowledge, I shall take it that knowledge purports to be subject to broadly articulable intellectual controls: for instance, that no proposition is ever true simply and solely because the putative knower wants to believe it, that canons of reasoning and evidence always apply and may be appealed to by researchers in support of or against the hypotheses being considered, and that bodies of knowledge must be coherent. These elementary constraints make it possible to appraise the efforts of educators and researchers—whether they reason well or badly, have done their homework for the specific project in question, and so on. These questions are all subject to objective investigation.

And so, I think, we can without serious distortion talk about education as, indeed, having a goal: to bring it about that the clients of educators know more, have an improved ability to recognize knowledge when they encounter it and an improved capacity to discover more of it. When we suppose that a given candidate for a position as an educator is preferable to another, given budgetary constraints, then it is in regard to that candidate's potential for promoting knowledge that we speak. It is to be supposed that that candidate's students would learn more, or that the candidate would produce better research, or some mix of the two, if the job goes to that one than to the other.

It might be insisted that the situation is different in the *public* sector of education. In that sector, the jobs available are allegedly devoted to tasks demanded by the public interest; and in a democratic country, one might hold, all have a right to be considered for the employments arising. This would create a tension between two very different considerations: the public's right to the most efficient provision of the service in question, and its right to equality of consideration in receiving the benefit of employment. But if the best people, in the judgment of public employers, are all from some specific sector of the populace, then the others will have been excluded from a benefit, which, *qua* public benefit, should be equally available to all. Which of these considerations should take precedence?

The answer is that public employment is *not*, as such, a "benefit" of the types that the public institutions in question are supposed to be supplying. The latter supply some benefit *from* their labors, indeed, and *that* is the one to which the public is entitled (if it is). Thus there is no credible case for insisting, as if it were a requirement of justice, that the employer randomize over all applicants for a particular job, either in general or with respect to any particular variable. Even public employers should, instead, hire whoever is most suitable from the point of view of performance. In the present case, what is in question is performance at promoting human knowledge, by teaching and research.

Nor is there a requirement to make certain that all possible applicants have been "fairly considered." An acquaintance in the philosophical profession was bemoaning his duty, as a member of the hiring committee of his department, to interview a couple of dozen candidates for an opening, winnowed down from over six hundred initial applicants. Any of those applicants, one gathers, is nowadays thought to have a right to fair consideration, and could even have made a legal case against the department concerned if evidence could be supplied that he (or rather, for all practical purposes nowadays, *she*) was passed over in favor of some "less qualified" person. To suppose this is to license what would in fact be an enormous waste of social resources, the rational basis for which is precisely nil. All selecting of candidates for anything is done against the constraint of a budget of resources to be devoted to it. Merely reading the complete dossiers of all those Ph.D.-holders is a good couple of weeks' work at, say, ten minutes per dossier—hardly adequate for a decent appreciation anyway. Multiply this by the number of members on the committee, add in still more hours of consideration by a department, factor in the immense number of hours spent by all those candidates filling out forms, and dollars spent photocopying, posting, and so on, and you have a formula for an immense amount of expensive time being spent on purposes which in themselves do not promote the goal of education. Committee time is not teaching time and it is not research time. If economy is not observed on the administrative front, then the educational purpose, which is the fundamental one, suffers. Factor in the enormous frustration, and enormous potential for wrangling over matters of intrinsically modest moment, and the point is sufficiently made. Justice cannot coherently be understood to require the expenditure of whatever resources it may take to find the one best candidate. The idea that there should be an enforceable duty underlying all this is one that does not recommend itself to the sober intellect. A supposedly academic establishment so constrained will produce litigation instead of knowledge, and second-rate lawyers rather than philosophers.

Nevertheless, the goals of education certainly call for getting the best person possible given the constraints of resources of time, money, and energy. Once our short list of candidates is assembled, and it is reasonably clear by educational criteria that candidate A is the best for the particular position being considered, then intervention to require the selecting of some other, on the basis of some criterion having no relation to the educational one, is not acceptable. But that is what any program of "affirmative action" will do. Of course it is possible that, say, gender or race should not be wholly extraneous; in those rare cases, those factors may contribute to one's qualification, just as, in choosing actors to play the leading male, males are usually the only ones to get serious consideration. But it would be idle to pretend that race, gender, and the like are typically relevant for any genuinely academic appointment. And insistence upon any such criterion is essentially certain to clash with the academic ones in any but the shortest of short runs.

On what grounds might it be thought that other than educational goals may legitimately outweigh educational ones at an ostensibly educational institution? Prevailing arguments, as we have seen, have nothing to be said for them. But what is more recently said takes us to a very different level or levels: specifically, to the earlier stages prior to university—the primary or secondary schools and the family. The former are alleged to be guilty of brainwashing little girls, say, into the view that they should not be worrying their cute little heads about such matters as mathematics and science, or of encouraging an atmosphere in which their peers do the same. And the lesser enrolment of women in the "hard" sciences is then attributed to this purely social cause. At the other end of the educational spectrum, there is the decreasing but still not nonexistent tendency of women to eschew out-of-home positions and devote themselves to domestic pursuits. Even now there are quite a few of those full-time mothers and homemakers to be found, though they are a modest minority. (Also not infrequently, the politically correct view ascribes this tendency to still more brainwashing by a sexist society.)

The socialization view of how girls come to prefer English to math, sociology to physics, is certainly disputable. Precisely how much schools had to do with it, and what if anything they should do about it, are eminently disputable. What is not disputable is that upon entry to university, the percentage of women who go into the sciences and engineering, is, by and large, very small compared to that of males, whereas in some areas of the humanities and social sciences, women often predominate. Likewise, the ratio of women to men in the more abstract or quantitatively oriented of the arts subjects, such as philosophy and economics, is comparatively smaller than in English and sociology. The result is that in many subjects, calls for equalization in faculty departments are unfulfillable in fact, no matter what any policymaker or theorist might like. In addition, the "employment pool" of women on the whole remains smaller than that of men, because of the still appreciable incidence of women who choose the domestic life over the professional one. The determined "egalitarian," who would like to see equality between the sexes in all occupations, is thus proposing a program that is necessarily unfulfillable, until such time as women cease to choose to become homemakers at all, and until whatever factors prompt women and men to enrol in the various academic subjects in unequal ratios cease to function.

Needless to say, these are not developments to be expected any time soon. Meanwhile, the questions are these: first, is the proposed goal of equality in all occupations by sex, etc., a rational goal for society? And second, even if it were, is it one that academia in particular should be trying to do something about? I have by implication argued against the first one already: it is not a lofty ideal but a silly one, which flies directly in the face of personal liberty—an ideal far more fundamental, and far more conducive to social prosperity and peace. As to the second, it has to be pointed out that by the time the student gets to university, it's *too late*. Selective preference for women or blacks or left-handeds or whatever is not going to do anything to "correct" the alleged damage, if that's what it was, from earlier levels. The university administrator and the university teacher must take what they can get, and to the best of their ability transmit to this material the virtues and goals of academia. Those goals concern knowledge, and not the restructuring of society vis-à-vis an enormous list of variables that have nothing particularly to do with it. To *study* and *discuss* such proposals is, of course, one of the things the academy should be doing. But that is hardly the same as embracing them without examination.

Despite all this, political correctness holds the day. So those women who do earn Ph.D.'s in the statistically more masculine subjects have the red carpet laid out for them—even though the areas in which women predominate, one might note, rarely make correspondingly intense, or any, effort to recruit males at the expense of females. In the typical case in which it is confessed that fifty-fifty splits, say, are an impossible goal," a structure more subversive because less obviously impossible is employed. In this subtler variation, it is observed that n percent of graduate students currently or recently studying in the discipline are, say, females. It is then decreed that the proper target is for a given department to match, in its teaching staff, that percentage over some modest time period, say a decade. And the result? In a great many fields, the number of women students has increased greatly over the past few decades—typically twice what it was three decades ago, and much greater than two decades ago. But in a university department with x members, normally more than half are tenured professors of long standing, hired when the number of women was much smaller. Gender-blind hiring therefore would (and did) lead to a much greater proportion of its staff now being male than the current proportion of graduate students in the field. Most of those aren't about to retire over the next decade. So in order to meet the allegedly fair target, the department in question will be obliged to take on virtually *no* males over the period during which it is to meet that target.

For example, suppose the department now has nine male and one female tenured professors, reflecting the fact that when they were hired, only one of ten Ph.D. candidates in that field was female; and perhaps they have three other nontenured staff, of which one is female. Meanwhile, 30 percent of the graduate students *now* in the field are women. To end up, over ten years, with 30 percent females on its professorial staff, it must have, by the end of that period, five women (4.9). And suppose it has three positions coming open in those ten years. How many of them will have to be taken by women, then? You guessed it: *all* of them!

By contrast, a policy of hiring exclusively on perceived merit in the hypothetical field in question would lead us, if the field's women are on average as capable as the men, to expect an average of about 30 percent women to be hired. The difference between the two *policies* is as night and day. Multiply the very typical case of my hypothetical 13-member department by hundreds in the United States and Canada alone, and then consider the whole set of graduate students hoping to achieve an academic career—and the arithmetic shows that affirmative action policies of an apparently quite "mild" kind are a recipe for disaster. The first form of it is assurance that a large portion of our academic resources, expended in training hopeful young males especially, will be wasted (a way of putting it that distracts from the human costs to those concerned.) For the second, we need to consider a different side effect. In the occasional department, a male or even two will be taken on. A bit of elementary arithmetic shows what will result. If from within each group the best are chosen, and 5 percent of the males and 90 percent of the females are hired from among a group with a random distribution of abilities, that rare male who does get a job is likely to be something close to a superstar by the standards of the field. The department in question will then be divided into two classes: women who have the entirely justified feeling that they were not hired on account of their merits, and the occasional male who was—and who in consequence towers over his distaff colleagues in the respects that any academic admires. This is hardly a formula for a happy or productive academic unit; nor is it unlikely to be noticed by students.

As we have seen, the supposition that such policies are only applied when the candidates are of ''approximately equal merit'' is in practice totally flouted anyway. Women without completed doctorates, no publications, and a field of concentration quite alien to what was wanted are routinely hired over male applicants with completed degrees, half a dozen publications, and a career in graduate school devoted to precisely the field advertised for. What used to be downright illegal, under the heading of discrimination, has become customary: advertisements make reference, at varying degrees of explicitness, to the sex or race of the applicant, and when they do not, applicants soon enough find out what is ''between the lines'' of the advertisements they did see. For contemporary male graduate students in the humanities, the message is clear: forget it! Stories of unemployed male Ph.D.'s who can paper the walls of their apartments with rejection notices, all with the same message—sorry, wrong sex!—are the literal truth nowadays, not fanciful inventions.

A public policy that is based on ignorance reinforced by statistical shenanigans, and on incoherent ideals of society, should not have the support of intelligent persons. To explain the prevalence of the ill-considered ideas of ''fairness'' officially touted on behalf of affirmative action, we must look in another direction. And what can that be? Persuasive answers are distressingly easy to come by. Affirmative action programs provide employment for administrators, both in governments and in our educational institutions. Administrators need know nothing about mathematics or philosophy if they have but to discern the gender of applicants. If that's all one needs to justify stepping in and reversing the judgments of accomplished academics in the field, the administrator is, to put it bluntly, in clover. And as to women themselves, of course, it can hardly be a great difficulty to see why someone might like to be in a situation where she is essentially assured of entry into a desirable profession if she is even minimally competent. (What competent women who would have been hired anyway think of it is quite another matter, of course. They made it on merit, and have no interest in being joined by people of less accomplishment hired on the basis of gender, race, or whatever.) But the standing logic of politics assures that the latter will be outweighed by the former. The logic of democracy is the logic of mediocrity supplied with arbitrary power.

Take a goodly dash of sophistry, add a generous helping of power politics, and you get the picture well enough. But if you seek a justification for affirmative action that has solid intellectual credentials and is consistent with the ideals of a liberal society, we can say the same thing as the administrator says to the aspiring but male contemporary Ph.D. graduate: Forget it!

Justice in Expression: When Does Speech "Harrass"?

The last question on our list concerns speech codes: whether various spoken or written utterances should be forbidden as deprecatory or otherwise harmful when they previously weren't so considered, or perhaps made illegal when they were formerly regarded as minor or trivial. At first glance, this seems more promising than any of the other proposals. Obviously people should not be free to inflict damages on each other, and if there can be verbal damages, then the case for limiting speech in those respects seems clear enough. Or does it?

Unfortunately, the category of "damage" is not so easy to define when verbal damage is the type in question. Sticks and stones have, in this regard, the advantage in court: broken bones are generally plain for all to see, and are agreed by all to be an evil. It is obviously false, as the old adage had it, that words, by contrast, can "never hurt." Of course they can. But here a problem of subjectivity really does come to the fore. Some people are "thick-skinned": words do not hurt them because they refuse to let them hurt. Others will be cast into inward turmoil by small talk, perhaps wounded for life. How much resistance to hurts of the kind in question may we expect of people? Can not people be hurt by words that ought not to hurt them? And just where does the claimed hurt lie? If a deeply religious person is exposed to familiar and powerful arguments against the existence of God, that person may well be offended and, yes, hurt. Yet if that person is enrolled in a university-level course in the philosophy of religion, what could he reasonably expect? In academia we must resolve, as a professional commitment, to "value the truth above our friends," as Aristotle put it.

We must follow the argument where *it* goes, not where *we* would *like it* to go. If this is sometimes painful, well, that's part of the intellectual life.

In the present climate, clearly, the thresholds for assessing hurt have been substantially lowered. In many times and places, the free exchange of insults was a normal part of the scene, and those who "couldn't take it" were invited to retreat and lick their wounds; they would scarcely dream of taking them to a lawyer, though they would, given the right physical equipment, often enough translate those wounds into blows. But how is the public, or anyone, to discern the proper exchange rate for words versus blows?

Such problems are characteristically soluble by *privatization:* that is, by establishing property rights over areas in which such exchanges take place, with clear rules applying to all who enter—clear, because (and if) they are provided by the person in charge, such as the houseowner. Provided those entering can freely leave, the imposition of the rules in those places is fair, and there is no fundamental problem. Potential brawlers in bars will know how much they can get away with—more in a bar known to be rough, less in a genteel establishment. Persons in a church service are not welcome to harangue the startled congregation with political diatribes, and random cries of "Fire!" in a crowded theatre are not welcome. A similar solution should be possible in colleges and universities, which are in principle free to establish their own codes of verbal decorum. But that solution is more problematic when the institution is state-owned, supposedly delivering its product, education, under a public mandate, to all persons capable of benefiting from it. When the public is a liberal public, as we now think all publics ought to be, then the question of finding the right rules for persons encountering each other in public places arises in acute form. The chief administrators cannot so easily just decide to adopt a certain code and let it go at that, if they suppose they are acting on behalf of the public, for public purposes. And for that matter, even at private institutions, the question of precisely who "owns" the place is not always easy to answer, nor would its trustees or senior administrators accept that they should lay down a law without consultation.

The present situation is greatly exacerbated by another phenomenon: the habit of insisting that certain claims are *inherently* demeaning to some group, independently of their cognitive credentials. Suppose that a certain group is, on average, significantly different from some other group, in respects to which considerable value is attached. For example, relative performance on standard IQ tests was a heated topic a couple of decades back. A great deal of evidence pointed to statistically significant differences among the races, and articles were written maintaining that this did not prove that the lowest-scoring race (the blacks) was inherently less intelligent than the others, or that the highest-scoring race (the Asians) was inherently more intelligent than they, and so on. It is interesting to consider why this was regarded as politically sensitive, when a similar fact about any *individual* would instead be regarded merely as an important piece of information about that individual's future prospects at certain undertakings, since it could plainly provide useful guidance concerning how that person might best direct his or her energies. Meanwhile, however, politics entered—and the utterance of what may well be true propositions has come to be regarded as equivalent to verbal abuse. Speakers proposing to present "controversial" theses to public audiences are then subjected to verbal abuse in the more usual sense of the term, and often to physical threats as well. How is a university community to maintain a level of decorum compatible with the peaceful pursuit of knowledge if the distinction between verbal abuse, on the one hand, and controversial scholarship, on the other, is not recognized and maintained? More difficult yet is the distinction between scholarly research and controversial recommendations for public policy. When the latter is proposed as being supported by the former, there is a tendency to decry the research in the course of decrying the policy—regardless of the scholarly merits of the research itself.

One helpful move, we might suppose, would be to insist on the hitherto familiar distinction between attacks on individuals, as such, and attacks on their doctrines. The latter are eligible for criticism, including scathing criticism. We are entitled to think a colleague's published views absurd, incoherent, baseless; but we may not accost him in the hall with personal invective. Even so, this is not entirely easy. If I think that your views about such-and-such are silly, do I not imply a deficiency in you—at least a lapse in your cognitive apparatus sufficient to generate the absurdity in question? Still, with effort, we manage to refrain from accosting people with their failings, even if our judgment is perfectly well taken. Philosophers do not call each other idiots, even while regarding their arguments or conclusions as idiotic. That is certainly as it should be.

The situation is worsened a good deal when characterization of large groups of humans is in question—as it frequently is these days. If we generalize about such a group, in particular in terms of some or other capacities in respect of which some large groups seem to differ significantly from others, and those capacities are valued or disvalued in some way, then a value judgment soon arises about the capacities of the group in question: *it* is labelled or associated with a deficiency if it is the group with, say, lower test scores or a lower incidence of success at whatever endeavors the capacity is useful for. At this point, making a factual claim, with however good evidence, is regarded as insult. The researcher who undertakes even to try to measure one of the variables in question is likely to be accused of racism, sexism, or whatever ism is currently favored.

There are, then, interesting and difficult problems in this area. But their very difficulty, amounting to something close to inherent impossibility, is precisely one of the chief factors contributing to the recent increase of administrative imposition in these exchanges. If it is impossible to say objectively whether x is or is not equal to y, and yet a legal requirement is imposed on A to render x to some group in an amount equal to y, then the most obvious way to handle the matter publicly is to appoint an arbitrator equipped with the power to *declare* that x is or is not equal to y in this case. There is no way to gainsay the word of the administrators, since no criteria exist for corroborating or refuting the claim—your word may be as good as theirs, but they are the ones with the power. And so power shifts from students, faculty, general employees, or ordinary citizens to administrators—from the people, in short, to their rulers. The power *has* to be arbitrary power, under the circumstances. And it is certain to be wielded by the incompetent: who, after all, is competent to do the impossible?

Consider the important related case of rape and its equivalent. Nobody condones what we used to have in mind by the term "rape." What we had in mind under that description were violent sexual actions, in which the word of the victim carried no weight with the assailant and the victim, to put it mildly, was not consulted by him. Now, however, it is held that if a woman invites a man up to her flat, engages in extensive sexual activities of a kind that he could reasonably construe as positively inviting intercourse, and then later *claims* that she refused, much to the surprise and mortification of her partner, we are now to understand that his action is rape—even though he didn't see it that way at all, and had no reason at the time to suppose she saw it that way either. Indeed, it could easily come about that all the facts of the case are agreed upon by both parties, and yet the decision as to whether it was rape must be made retroactively by judge and jury. This is hardly what people had in mind in classifying rape as a serious, violent crime. But the penalties, which were established on the earlier assumptions and therefore appropriately severe, continue to be visited on those convicted.

The example of rape is neighbor to another major field of proposed intervention along political correctness lines: "harassment," especially of the sexual variety. What is especially significant about recent talk about this is that, as with rape, the kind of activity normally and originally meant by the term is very different from what is now intended. Here's the OED entry:

> harass: (1) To wear out, tire out, or exhaust with fatigue, care, trouble, etc.; (2) to harry, lay waste, devastate, plunder; (3) to trouble or vex by repeated attacks; (4) to trouble, worry, distress with annoying labour, care, perplexity, importunity, misfortune, etc.; (5) to scrape or rub.

In all these, the emphasis is on *repeated* incursions which wear down the victim, the whole sequence ultimately inflicting major damage. This central idea, however, is essentially abrogated in new harassment legislation. Now a single remark is enough to get the alleged assaulter up for a charge of harassment. And in the case where the purported victim is of some politically recognized minority, her (or, more rarely, his) word on the matter is accorded far more weight than would be the word of anyone not a member of some recognized "minority." Here's an example. "The Government of Ontario has adopted a policy of zero tolerance of harassment and discrimination at Ontario's universities . . . "[14]; a few pages later, we read the following, under "Definitions and examples":

> Harassment—one or a series of vexatious comments or conduct related to one or more of the prohibited grounds that is known or might reasonably be known to be unwelcome/unwanted, offensive, intimidating, hostile, or inappropriate. [Examples mentioned include gestures, remarks, jokes, taunting, innuendo . . .][15]

The result of all this is that, again, essentially arbitrary power has flowed to those claiming to be victims and thus to the administrators of the law or rule in question. This creates a new class of victims, victims of the law, or of the campus administration, as the case may be—victims whose cases are simply not recognized, rather than weighed on their merits. And the idea that punishments should fit crimes is also cast to the four winds. People lose university positions, students are ejected from colleges, because of isolated remarks that happen to offend someone. Or when they are able to resist, they are ground down financially in their efforts to defend themselves.

We are caught, especially in the academy, between potentially conflicting interests here. On one hand, insult, verbal abuse such as name-calling, and offensive remarks are in general to be avoided, and the threshold of unacceptable behavior is lowish. On the other hand, we are interested in the truth. There the indicated principle is that very few holds are barred. Complicating our thought about the first is that a great deal of what makes ordinary conversational speech pleasurable is, when one thinks of it, construable as abusive, certainly as aggressive, in some way or other. Friends who would die for each other nevertheless rib each other mercilessly: Poles, Scandinavians, Newfoundlanders, Jews—to name but a few from a vast array—have been the butt of jokes, and often enough tell them on themselves, even become connoisseurs. And, frankly, a lot of those jokes are genuinely hilarious. The ability to laugh at ourselves is often cited as one of the distinguishing marks of humanity, and for good reason; even when we laugh at each other, so long as the terms are reasonably reciprocal and done under a general understanding of friendliness, it's a good thing. Those who want to put a damper on the potential aggression in speech run a danger of putting a damper on one of the major pleasures of life for many people, a pleasure by no means exclusive to academics and intellectuals. And when the proposed threshold of acceptability is set at zero, as it too often is,[16] we don't just have a "damper"—we have something more in the nature of a steamroller.

I previously suggested that privatization offers hope of a rational, general solution to these problems. The most useful approach to these controversies is to take that down to the level of individual speech interactions in more or less public spaces. There is, I suggest, one that stands out above anything else: the *hearer* must have the same liberty as the *speaker*. If your audience is unwilling, then it must be free, and easily able, to avoid the offensive speech. If neither of those conditions is realized, then the speaker must desist, upon realizing that his or her speech-act is definitely unwanted. The point of objecting to *harassment*, properly so called, is that it violates this principle: the victim cannot get away, the harasser continues at high volume, follows him around, phones him repeatedly, and so on. Yet if whatever you say, regardless of how infrequently you say it, is automatically "harassment," then the alleged harasser has nothing to go on. Now it is he who can't get away from the "speech police," who are entitled to act on virtually no evidence—and will hound him right out of academia, or wherever. Who now is harassing whom?

A useful approximation to privatization is to designate parts of public areas for special purposes with corresponding speech rules. In a study area or during a concert, no speech at all is the right amount; but in a cafeteria, cacophony is normal. Sensible rules are not hard to come by, and corresponding methods and levels of enforcement not difficult.

We must remember that what's wrong with abuses, including speech abuses, is that they hurt particular people. An offender owes something to his victim—but rarely very much. An apology is usually sufficient, and we may with profit suggest a version of the golden rule as our guide: would you, the putative victim, object to being bundled out of school, losing your job, or being forced to spend thousands in legal fees, for inflicting a comparable injury on someone else? A driver who smashes up someone's car at an intersection suffers the loss of a bit of time, a modest deductible, and a slight increase in insurance rates, and little else, despite the very considerable real damage and nuisance inflicted. Should someone who insults you by calling you by a selection of your least favorite ethnic epithets be called to greater account? And what if he backs down when you indignantly respond, offering apology in the process? A speech code is sure to be unresponsive to the latter, and unthinking about the former.

Speech, let us remember, is a major facilitator and a highly valued component of social intercourse. It is, moreover, enormously fluid, subtle, adaptable, rich in ambiguity, unkempt, and untamed. Precisely specifying its limits is not possible, and whoever proposes to do so must be looked on with suspicion. Not allowing grown people to say things to other grown people is so fraught with peril, so threatening to the social benefits speech makes possible, that when due allowance is made, one should soberly conclude that for the generality of cases, the best speech *code* is none at all. Forced apology is as far as it should go.

If we turn to the classroom and the public forum, different considerations come into view. The main thing is relevance to the subject matter of the course or inquiry. Classrooms are not to be used as platforms for the preaching of pet ideologies or hobbies not germane to the purported subject, for example—though public nonacademic forums lack even that restriction. But once within that important bound, no further restrictions may properly be imposed on the range of hypotheses to be considered—though plenty are to be imposed in the way of intellectual discipline in their consideration. Here if anywhere, the fact that something is unpopular, that students or teachers don't *want* to believe a proposition, is never sufficient reason for disallowing someone from proposing it. By contrast, that the speaker has no evidence, or his proposal doesn't make any sense, must count strongly. In the academy, we all are present voluntarily, to confront the world around us with as clear an eye as possible. In it, Mill's celebrated defense of free speech reigns supreme.[17]

Here is where the expression "political correctness" comes crucially into relation with the central purposes of the academy. The connotation of that expression is precisely that a proposition is to be believed because one's believing it promotes some political program—and one whose credentials in its own right simply don't pass muster. In the end, what political correctness basically seems to tell us is that p is true because the right people say it is. A genuine academy cannot thrive under such a regime. Nor, I think, can a society.

Why Political Correctness?

The first axiom of good government is that it is to be government in the interests of the governed, not those of the governors; and of *all* the governed, not just selected portions at the expense of the rest. In this sense, certainly, government must be "equal." But the equality concerned is the equal right to live as one chooses, given one's resources. It is not the equal right that others provide you with just as much of some good as anyone else, or to extort the maximum from the rest. The ideology of political correctness serves to inflate the claims of some of the governed against others of them, and then to inflate the power of the governors in the process of "correcting" the alleged imbalance. In the preceding chapters, I have tried to detail how this happens in each case, and to expose how the apparently plausible, even innocuous, premises invoked by the proponents of political correctness are subtly distorted into mockeries of those familiar principles, and how at a minimum they ignore or fly in the face of empirical evidence.

Let us survey our results. The critics of "canonical" bodies of literature want all literature to be regarded as equal regardless of perceived merit, or insist that we practice what amounts to affirmative action for the previously noncanonical. But while all literature has an equal right to *exist*, there is no basis whatever for supposing that all literature is *equal*, or that canons of literary criticism are baseless or somehow demeaning to the selections they rate as less worthy; and there is, on the contrary, ample reason for supposing that there really is great literature and great art, or seminal and important literature and art that is worth studying and holding up as canonical, while never excluding other works from consideration.

Likewise there is, of course, no exclusion of literary and artistic works from all cultures; but the politically correct view would have it that we should be devoting something like "equal time" to the works of all cultures—which is both impossible and pointless. We are who we are, and we quite properly look at the world from our own corner of it. From this perspective, the liberal intellect needs to know that there are other and very different ways of life and expression, and to extend sympathetic attention to selected bits of it. Period.

Postmodernism and deconstruction, in turn, virtually affirm that all sentences are equal, none having any greater claim to "truth" than any other, because there is no truth or, what comes to the same thing, because truth is what you make it on the basis of political beliefs and practices. Those high-flown conceits are incapable of being coherently expounded, and provide no basis whatever for an effective critique of anything.

Affirmative action is perhaps the most widely-invoked politically correct practice. It also begins with the perfectly reasonable view that we should not, in our hiring practices, exclude anyone on the basis of race, gender, and other normally irrelevant features—but then warps that sensible dictum into the completely unsupported and ultimately incoherent conclusion that we should give strong preference in employment to members of supposedly oppressed or previously oppressed groups, despite clear criteria of merit in the field, criteria that have no particular connection to the claimed or even actual oppressions to which these policies allegedly respond. The view subtly converts to an ideological agenda, demanding that employees in each particular employment are about equally distributed by those very factors in relation to the population as a whole. Again, the goal is impossible, incoherent, and arbitrary—while providing a field day for authority figures.

Finally, in considering the category of offensive speech, we found an alleged disparity in the power of speakers to inflict "verbal damage" converted into a very real disparity in the powers of supposed or erstwhile victims of such damage, with, again, a corresponding expansion of the powers of administrators to inflict major evils on the supposed harassers.

These are diverse areas, but a common thread runs through them: in each case, the policy, program, or principle so described works to the ostensible benefit of some or other group within the relevant populace, but clearly at the expense of another group, does so independently of the demonstrated merit of persons in the beneficiary group, and does so in a way that tends to politicize issues and to centralize power. All of the proposed policies work to the greater power of centralized authority, by requiring substantial administration, including especially substantial policing, adjudicative, and punishing activity. Political correctness policies create whole new legions of "bad guys," to whom are attributed evil but empirically undetectable motives: If you're male, or white, or whatever, you're automatically guilty, no matter what you've actually done. And so it creates legions of police—"thought police," as a current expression all too accurately has it—alongside the other administrators, to hunt down and combat the newly identified witches. Of course the cost of all this is borne by us all in general, as well as by the newly identified bad guys in particular.

Some of the costs are financial. When a university sets up a new "human rights office," with its sexual harassment officer, secretaries, and so on, it devotes hundreds of thousands, even millions of dollars to nonacademic ends—money that might better have been spared the taxpayer and/or the student, or else spent on what universities are actually for, such as on books, research, laboratories, or forums on subjects with intellectual content. It might have been said, in more halcyon days, "What's a hundred thousand out of a budget of fifty million?" The answer now can often be put quite precisely: the entirety of that university's library holdings in early Renaissance philosophy, the opportunity to acquire the papers of some important scientist in the past, the entire performing arts series of the university for a full year, one entire faculty position in a subject no longer taught because the department concerned can no longer afford to offer it, and so on. But other of the costs, especially in lessened opportunities to learn by future students, more restricted opportunities to think and write by future researchers, will of course be impossible to compute precisely.

The thrust of political correctness, in short, is against individual freedom and academic efficiency, and for centralized control. No doubt the control is democratic: that is, the familiar political machinery grinds out the programs in question. In all likelihood, an unsuspecting or unknowing public inadvertently supported those who came up with these policies, in the course of trying to do something else. The benefits of the academy in particular, as perhaps of liberty in general, are not immediately obvious to the voter; the voice of the demagogue, on the other hand, reaches him loud and, as he thinks, clear. In any case, we should hardly be happier about the Nazis when we learn that they were voted into office.

My coauthor and I wrote down our thoughts independently, apart from general agreement on the issues to be discussed, and exposure to early and tentative partial drafts. I look forward to seeing her case for a range of policies that I have argued to be pretty thoroughly deplorable. It will be interesting to see whether I am persuaded of a need to reduce the strength of my indictment on the basis of her essay, brief response to which will follow.

Notes

1. See Charles A. Thomas, Jr., Kary B. Mullis, and Phillip E. Johnson, "What Causes AIDS?" in *Reason,* June, 1994, pp. 18–23.

2. Molefi Kete Asante, "Multiculturalism: an Exchange," in *Debating P.C.,* ed. Paul Berman (New York: Dell, 1992), pp. 299–311; quote, p. 303.

3. See my own addition to the vast literature on relativism: "Reflections on Moral Relativity," Critical Notice of David Wong, *Moral Relativity, Canadian Journal of Philosophy* 17, no. 1 (1987): 235–257.

4. Twenty-second Conference on Value Inquiry, Drew University, New Jersey, April 1993.

5. Thomas Hobbes, *Leviathan:* Ch. XV—Law V. [many editions]

6. J. S. Mill, *Utilitarianism,* Chapter Two. [many editions]

7. Berman, *Debating P.C.,* p. 114.

8. Stephen White, *Political Theory and Postmodernism* (Cambridge, U.K.: Cambridge University Press, 1991), p. 15.

9. *Ibid.,* p. 16.

10. *Ibid.,* p. 27.

11. See Walter Block and Michael W. Walker, *Focus: On Employment Equity* (Vancouver and Toronto: Fraser Institute, 1985), especially Chap. 4, "A Statistical Analysis of Discrimination," pp. 41–62.

12. The example describes an actual case, not a hypothetical one.

13. The author's more thorough analysis of the arguments concerning discrimination may be found in *Moral Matters* (Peterborough, Ontario: Broadview Press, 1993), Chap. 12, and "Is Discrimination Unjust?," in Wil Waluchow & Deborah Poff, *Business Ethics in Canada* (Prentice-Hall, 1987; 2nd ed., 1991).

14. "Framework Regarding Prevention of Harassment and Discrimination in Ontario Universities," circulated by the Ontario Ministry of Education and Training in Ontario universities in winter 1994, p. 1.

15. *Ibid.,* p. 4.

16. Example: The aforementioned document (cf. note 14) opens with these words: "The Government of Ontario has adopted a policy of zero tolerance of harassment and discrimination at Ontario's universities . . ."

17. In case any reader is not familiar with this canonical work of western thought, the source is J. S. Mill, *On Liberty,* Chap. 2. [There are innumerable editions and anthology excerpts.]

Response

Marilyn Friedman

Jan Narveson and I agree on a number of points. We both believe, to
borrow his words, that the Western canon is not hallowed terrain; it is a
somewhat loose and unruly collection of works that, while important,
brilliant, or germinal, should not be called the best works. The canon is
"shot through with judgments of value." There are, furthermore, no
common cross-cultural standards for making meaningful comparisons
between the literary or artistic products of diverse cultures; all standards
for evaluating cultural works are culturebound. Liberal education, however, should aim at comprehensiveness; this is best done by both exploring works from Western culture and becoming acquainted with works
from other cultures. There are several good reasons for Westerners to
study non-Western cultures; Westerners might actually learn something
and might better understand those in Western societies who hail from
non-Western cultures. In addition, the academic environment should be
one of civility. Speakers should desist from unwanted, offensive speech
in such settings as classrooms and public forums if the audience is not
easily able to avoid hearing the speech in question. As to Professor
Narveson's joke course on "Western Barbarism"—I wish I had thought
of that myself.

Beyond these few reasonable ideas, Professor Narveson makes many
dubious claims. For him, political correctness in general connotes a
perspective according to which "truth" is what is believed by the
"right people," all literature is "equal" regardless of genuine merit,
all issues are political, dissenters should be policed and punished, and
white males are guilty no matter what they do. He charges that the
ultimate politically correct goal of equality is a confusion serving to
mask an underlying "*ressentiment.*" My earlier discussion suggests
that these depictions of political correctness are caricatures.[1] In the

pages that follow, I will respond in four areas. First, I dispute some of Professor Narveson's miscellaneous charges. Second, I defend affirmative action. Third, I dispel further misunderstandings of feminism. Fourth, I add a brief postscipt.

Miscellaneous

Professor Narveson sees confusion in the politically correct (PC) notion that "everything is political." This is indeed a confused notion—but it is not the typical PC view. The more widespread politically correct view about politics is that no area of human thought, inquiry, or scholarship is inherently immune to political biases or influences. Even the research projects of molecular chemistry could be influenced by politics, for example, by governmental efforts to build an arsenal of chemical weapons. Bias, as I observed earlier, does not necessarily produce false research results. Truthful results, however, may be lopsided, leaving many important matters uninvestigated and manifesting a limited range of possible research methods and paradigms.

Although politicizing something traditionally meant *making* it political, it has also come to mean *revealing* the political nature of something. When PC proponents say they are politicizing an already political domain of knowledge, they mean that they are revealing the political biases and influences in that domain. In this sense, to depoliticize something is to mask or hide its political nature. The confusion that Professor Narveson sees in the current use of these terms disappears on this interpretation. And politics, in PC discussions of it, is a comprehensive notion, referring not just to governmental processes but to any dimension of power or authority in social relationships.

PC advocates often claim that the Western canon and its research traditions and methods are pervaded by masculine and other biases. Professor Narveson ridicules the idea that the Western tradition might be founded on male collusion or a grand masculine conspiracy. These notions make no sense to Professor Narveson; scholars have no obvious reasons for rejecting quality works on irrelevant grounds.

The exclusion of women from academic and cultural life, however, to continue with this example, was not simply a matter of scholars devaluing works done by females. Rather, whole social institutions systematically excluded women *en masse* from formal education and professional activities (even while allowing the exploitation of lower-class women's physical labor). Before the laws of this century made a minimal level of education compulsory for girls as well as boys, women were routinely denied access to formal education even as the numbers of their educated brothers increased steadily.

Consider art history in particular. From the time of their inception in the late sixteenth century until the late nineteenth century, British and European art academies barred women from life-drawing classes (except as models) and, thus, from critical formal training in drawing the nude. Until the art academies began to lose importance in this century, this deprivation alone virtually precluded women from creating works of art that critics would consider great. It consigned female painters to such "minor" fields as portraiture and still life.[2] The few women who managed against all odds to create works of great aesthetic merit under these conditions needed to have more than simply the gift of surpassing genius. They needed to be born to middle- or upper-class wealth and to have unusual fathers who would engage serious private tutoring even for their daughters.

Professor Narveson is on the right track in thinking that the notion of a male conspiracy is the wrong explanation for this canonical history. It is certainly an incomplete explanation; it suggests that the exclusion of women from public culture was wholly the result of a deliberate plot by a small gang of vicious hypermisogynists. The male bias of the Western canon arose, rather, because of a widely accepted, deeply pervasive pattern of cultural practices that got most women married (and then, because of primitive or nonexistent contraceptive means, repeatedly pregnant) and also kept them out of public cultural life. It seems reasonable to guess that these practices were tolerated, if not supported outright, by many women as well as by most men. (What choice did women have?)

The role of individual male conspiracy, however, should not be completely discounted. All formal bars to women's participation in literary or artistic activity could only have been created and implemented by certain men, namely, those with decision-making power over cultural and educational institutions—the "gatekeepers of culture," to borrow a current phrase. The all-male canon in Western philosophy, for well over two millenia, relentlessly intoned one prominent public excuse for this exclusion: women's inferior rational capacities.

This sad historical sketch does not logically entail anything about contemporary literary or artistic attitudes toward women. Unfortunately, however, the Western canons that we inherit today date from bygone eras and are therefore dominated by the works of the infamous dead white men. How shall we deal with this imbalance? Precisely by counterbalancing the Western canon with cultural studies of works by women and members of other previously excluded groups. Professor Narveson is wrong, however, to think that this PC solution calls for a new canon with ''proportional representation'' of those groups. That notion makes no sense. Proportional to what?

My earlier discussion suggested no proportional guidelines for mixing multicultural studies with traditional Western studies (which I also urged that we retain). There is, I maintained, no principled way to decide *exactly* how to allocate culture studies so as to produce a well-educated citizenry for a genuinely just democratic polity. Autonomous faculty communities, deliberating together in light of contemporary cultural debates (such as appear in this volume), should be left to balance the components of their own curriculum for themselves—just as they now balance the other general education requirements in natural science, social science, and the rest.

What about the value of non-Western cultures? Professor Narveson accuses PC advocates of arguing that all cultures are equally legitimate and equally worthy of study; each has a right to our attention. His rejection of this view has two main parts. First, because there are no common, cross-cultural standards for comparing cultures or their literary traditions, there is therefore no foundation for the claim that all cultures are equally legitimate and equally worthy of study. Second, while there are prudent and wise reasons for Westerners to study non-Western cultures, such cultures have no *right* to be studied, no basis for claiming that Westerners *ought* to study them.

Professor Narveson's first concern is misplaced. The PC point is not that all cultures are, in some positively defensible sense, equally legitimate or equally valuable. Political correctness arose as a challenge to the common Western assumption that Western culture and European-centered literatures and perspectives are globally the best. Advocates of PC reject that pro-Western view precisely on the grounds that Professor Narveson articulates, namely, that there are no established cross-cultural standards for judging the merits of cultures or literary traditions. This rejection of the presumed universal superiority of Western culture is precisely what paves the way for defending multicultural studies.

Professor Narveson's second concern, that non-Western cultures have no *right* to the attention of Westerners, is also debatable. To say that Westerners *ought* to study non-Western cultures and marginalized Western subgroups is not necessarily to say that those cultures or groups have a *right* to be studied. Not all PC advocates think in terms of rights and even those who do might not advocate the odd notion of a ''right to be studied." The fact that a particular culture does not have a right to be studied, however, does not entail that we, therefore, have no responsibility to study it.

Professor Narveson concedes that it is "prudent" and "wise" for Westerners to study other cultures; after all, persons of different cultures are in "our" midst. I agree wholeheartedly that such studies are prudent and wise—and think that an even stronger claim is defensible. Who, after all, is this "we" whose "midst" it is supposed to be? The United States and Canada are both fundamentally pluralistic societies at their cultural roots and human origins, even if not in their operative political traditions. Members of these societies, like all human beings, have the moral obligation to treat other persons respectfully and to make sure that we are not oppressing, exploiting, abusing, or dominating others.

Our lives are interconnected with large numbers of others through various social, political, economic, and cultural relationships. History has amply shown us that these relationships have been the sites of historic patterns of exploitation and domination, even by unwitting participants. One preeminent means for ensuring that we are not unwittingly oppressing or exploiting others is to try to understand others as full human beings with their own points of view, especially those others whom history has shown that we are likely to oppress or exploit through the institutions in which we participate. This is just the sort of understanding promoted by studying the cultural works of other groups or communities, works that present something of the perspectives, histories, and circumstances of those groups. Thus it emerges that multicultural education, while not a categorical moral responsibility in its own right, is one important means for achieving something that *is* a categorical moral responsibility (if anything is): the respectful treatment of other persons.

In addition, our society is surely obligated as a whole to its younger generations to give them the best education it can afford to provide. We, in the United States, can certainly afford to provide a substantial component of cross-cultural and subcultural studies at all educational levels. We owe this to our younger generations if we are to raise them to be responsible and productive members of our multicultural society and the global community. Thus, where Professor Narveson sees multicultural studies merely as a "prudent" and "wise" educational policy, I see it as a matter of societal responsibility.

On the subject of speech, Professor Narveson agrees with PC advocates that vicious speech is inappropriate in public forums and classrooms. His treatment of this issue, however, is potentially misleading. In the context of discussing sexual harassment and hate speech, he urges that the search for truth should be allowed to proceed wherever it leads and should not be hampered by the fact that some of us may not like the conclusions that emerge from that pursuit. He claims, for example, that the currently low "thresholds for assessing hurt" could conflict with the search for truth.

Unfortunately, Professor Narveson's discussion merges two distinct issues: hateful or harassing speech, on one hand, and on the other, research results that present a derogatory picture of certain groups of people, for example, race-based IQ studies. This merger mistakenly suggests that the PC objection to verbal sexual harassment and hate speech is really nothing more than an overreaction by hypersensitive types to scholarly research results that they happen to find unpleasant.

It is true that some research results, such as those purporting to show race differences in IQ or sex differences in cognitive ability, have been hotly debated as gender and race issues. Verbal sexual harassment and hate speech, however, are not matters of debatable scholarship. Those who defend hate speech codes are not thereby calling for the suppression of unpleasant, but otherwise reputable, research results. Hateful and harassing speech are problems of communication, and therefore, problems in the interpersonal relationships that go on in academic (and other) communities.

About that problem of debatable scholarship: there is, to be sure, a moral problem with the publication of research results that demean people, especially groups of people with a history of being socially devalued. Researchers who uncover such results might well have individual moral responsibilities not to publicize them. (One wonders why those researchers are so intent on comparing population IQs or whatever in the first place.) At the very least, group-demeaning research should have to pass stricter scrutiny and be judged by higher standards than ordinary, nondemeaning research, since it is more likely than the latter to be distorted by covert, group-based prejudices. So long as research results are presented in a noninsulting manner and in a way that allows strict scrutiny and debate over their merits, however, then even group-demeaning research should not, in general, be suppressed.

There is no way to contain within reasonable bounds a policy of suppressing research that presents a demeaning portrait of some persons. What counts as demeaning, and to whom, are easily contested notions. The practical results of trying to suppress demeaning research is likely to be the suppression of the very people whom PC proponents would want to protect. Some white critics would be only too happy to suppress Afrocentrism as a perspective that they think demeans whites and Western culture, and some antifeminists would like to do the same to feminist research on rape, battering, and sexual harassment, which they think shows resentment toward men. Misguided as they are, these charges nevertheless reveal the obvious risks inherent in any general policy of research suppression.

It is, of course, legitimate to call for an end to *methodologically bad* research, and there is no reason to assume in advance that all studies of intelligence and cognitive capacities are methodologically sound. It is also appropriate to suggest in public debate that individual researchers are morally irresponsible for *publicizing* research results that demean oppressed groups, however methodologically flawless the underlying research might be. There should, however, be no government-enforced censorship of any type of research or cultural work that is otherwise legal to carry out—and this is a view that most, if not all, PC proponents would endorse.

On the topic of rape, Professor Narveson worries that the concept of rape is being stretched to cover behavior that is not rape at all. He suggests that men are being convicted of rape for situations in which the woman engaged "in extensive sexual activities of a kind that [the man] could reasonably construe as positively inviting intercourse." Professor Narveson does not cite any actual convictions or imprisonment for such cases, and there is good reason to doubt their existence. In any case, of *actual* rape convictions, we should always ask: in whose judgment were the sexual activities "extensive"? And, more importantly, from whose perspective did they "reasonably" and unambiguously "invite intercourse"?

These questions take us to the heart of the dispute between adversaries in a rape charge. Feminist legal studies have uncovered the historic tendency of courts to disbelieve women as witnesses in their own rape trials, women who claimed that they did not invite intercourse or consent to it.[3] In rape trials, perhaps more than elsewhere, the judicial standard of the "reasonable man" has revealed its covert gender-specific meaning. Only when black men were accused of raping white women, did women become highly credible witnesses—from the objectionably racist standpoint of white juries. Apart from those cases, the relevant standard for deciding what actually transpired between a particular man and a woman who accused him of rape has seldom been the standard of the "reasonable woman."

Feminism has sought to shift the balance of judicial credibility toward women as witnesses. As the balance shifts, a few isolated cases might indeed turn up in which (white) men are convicted for rape on the basis of weak rape accusations by (white or nonwhite) women. Faulty convictions are a hazard for any sort of criminal charge and should always be opposed. There is no reason, however, to think that the faulty rape conviction rate has become worse than it ever was or worse than it is for other felonies. In any case, this risk does not minimize the also-pressing need to improve the credibility of women as rape victims.

I will have more to say about feminism in the final part of this commentary. Before that: affirmative action.

Affirmative Action

Professor Narveson's critique of affirmative action can be summarized this way: the evidence does not show that groups such as blacks and women have really experienced the sort of employment discrimination for which affirmative action might be an appropriate remedy; and even if they have, affirmative action would still be a poor remedy. It fails to accomplish anything just in its own right, so it is not (morally) obligatory. At the same time, it is economically inefficient and it inflicts its own positive injustices by requiring businesses and educational institutions to adopt behavior that they do not desire to adopt. Thus, affirmative action is not only not (morally) required; it is also positively (morally) wrong.

What can the defender of affirmative action say in response to this view? To begin with, we should note that, in the realm of employment, the term ''affirmative action'' covers a wide array of practices, not all of which are equally vulnerable to Professor Narveson's objections. The general notion of affirmative action is that of positive action taken on behalf of a group that has been previously subjected to substantial employment discrimination—positive action beyond mere compliance with antidiscrimination law. The rationale for affirmative action is that, given the history of oppression and employment discrimination experienced by groups such as blacks and women, justice in the workplace will not sufficiently be realized merely by legislating against discrimination in employment decisions made from now on.[4] Some form of positive action is necessary in order to rectify that workplace injustice.

In actual practice, affirmative action programs encompass a variety of types of positive action. The most hotly debated policies are the governmentally mandated requirements that preference be given in hiring or promotion to members of designated groups. Often this preference is made a standing employment policy, thus potentially applying to some situations in which members of the designated groups are not the top candidates according to traditional forms of worker assessment.

This last point needs to be stated carefully. No affirmative action program requires the hiring or promotion of unqualified candidates. Nevertheless, within the realm of candidates who are at least minimally qualified, affirmative action programs might require decision procedures that circumvent or override traditional practices for determining the *most* qualified candidates. Here is where the "other things equal" policy, challenged by Professor Narveson, comes into play. Affirmative action programs commonly call for the hiring or promotion of certain group members when other things, such as traditional measures of job qualification, are approximately equal. These types of programs may be called "reverse-preferential" affirmative action policies.

It is important to reiterate that there is more to affirmative action than simply reverse-preferential employment policies. Affirmative action often involves, for example, job advertising carefully targeted at designated groups, special job training opportunities for members of designated groups, and efforts to eliminate group-based prejudice from the work environment. In the academic field, the era of affirmative action has yielded the anonymous refereeing of essays submitted for publication to professional journals as well as widely publicized job listings to counteract the secretive "old boy" networks that used to be prime sources of candidate recruitment. These latter practices are examples of positive action that has been undertaken to rectify academic workplace discrimination.

There is also an important distinction to be made between voluntary and mandated forms of affirmative action. When businesses or schools adopt affirmative action policies voluntarily, those policies obviously do not coercively interfere with the choices that decisionmakers would otherwise make—no more so than does any other policy set by management or democratically chosen by faculty senates. The most controversial form of affirmative action is that which involves governmental rules that *mandate* employment preferences for members of unfairly treated groups. It is crucial to remember that even if this form of affirmative action is wrong or misguided, nevertheless, other forms might well be perfectly permissible—or even morally required. Affirmative action as such should not be dismissed in one fell swoop; each type of affirmative action should be considered in terms of its own specific features.

Even mandated, reverse-preferential affirmative action must be carefully understood. Few, if any, affirmative action programs are mandated unconditionally. They are not imposed by government in a way that is unavoidable for employers, as, for example, would be the case if Congress were to make it a federal crime for any employer simply to lack an affirmative action program. Instead, most mandated affirmative action programs are mandated conditionally. They are imposed by government only on those employers who meet certain *avoidable* conditions.

The earliest federal mandates for affirmative action programs in the United States came from executive orders that required that a company have a reverse-preferential affirmative action program as a condition of doing business with the federal government.[5] Granted that, under this directive, a company would have to forgo a source of profit in order to avoid having an affirmative action program, nevertheless, the mandate is still avoidable without legal penalty, and that point is important. A financial disadvantage, or, more carefully, the loss of a potential customer, is a far cry from criminal sanctions; hence my term, "conditionally mandated."

It is important to bear in mind that most, if not all, employment-related, reverse-preferential affirmative action in the United States is of the conditionally mandated sort. This is the type that I support below. These policies have been defended in various ways over the past several decades, for example:

1. as compensation for past histories of group-based employment discrimination (compensation defense)
2. as rectification for the still-lingering effects of past discrimination (lingering effects defense)
3. as a counterbalance to the persistent unfair biases that continue to influence employment practices (persistent bias defense)
4. as recognition that being a woman or a member of an oppressed minority group can sometimes be a positive job qualification (revised qualifications defense)

These lines of argument are not equally strong or persuasive. The compensation and the lingering effects defenses, in particular, have been plausibly criticized.[6] In my estimation, the two best defenses of conditionally mandated, reverse-preferential affirmative action are the latter two arguments, the persistent bias and the revised qualifications defenses.

According to the persistent bias rationale, the goal of reverse-preferential affirmative action is to ensure genuinely fair employment practices. Mere antidiscrimination legislation by itself does not bring an end to unfairly discriminatory attitudes or practices. Both the personal attitudes of employment decision makers and the procedures they use to make employment decisions may remain biased against certain population groups, even without the conscious or explicit knowledge of those who make the decisions. Employment decision makers are ordinary, imperfect people who can misjudge job candidates and be oblivious to their own unconscious biases. Such attitudes and procedures are likely to persist and influence employment practices unless we take positive action to counteract them.

This approach is particularly relevant to employment selection processes that involve subjective judgments. Whenever a candidate is judged on the merits of her interviewing performance, the quality of her published work, or her likability as a coworker, for example, there is room for unconscious bias to cloud the assessments made by employment decision makers. A large body of evidence suggests, on balance, that in certain important employment-related areas, women's competences and achievements are generally ranked lower (by both women and men) than identical male competences and achievements.[7] Research indicates analogously that race plays a role in performance evaluation; both black and white evaluators rate members of their own race significantly more highly than members of the other race.[8] Since white employment decision makers outnumber blacks by a wide margin in the United States, the overall discriminatory impact on blacks is obvious.

The persistent biases defense, which I have been discussing, does not challenge traditional conceptions of merit, but merely calls for certain procedures to guard against group-based biases that might covertly contaminate traditional assessments. The revised qualifications defense goes one step further than this by redefining the standards traditionally used to assess candidate merit in some fields. In particular, membership in a previously discriminated-against group can sometimes be a positive job qualification. A minority-group teacher, for instance, can be an important role model for all students and might supply a perspective otherwise missing from a predominantly white faculty. Employment candidates with those traits should therefore earn extra merit points that boost their relative merit rankings. Taken together, the persistent bias and the revised qualifications defenses hold that the purpose of reverse-preferential affirmative action programs is to promote fair employment practices by ensuring that assessment standards are genuinely adequate to jobs and are not applied in a biased manner.

Professor Narveson questions the view that significant biases persist in employment practices. First, he challenges the idea that the underrepresentation of a particular group in a particular employment context is evidence of bias against that group in that context. In Professor Narveson's view, there is no reason to assume that talents for any given field are equally distributed among all population groups. Thus, no mere statistics about the small number of people of group G who hold jobs in industry Q tell us anything about whether or not G-type persons have experienced unfair group-based discrimination in that industry.

We do not, however, begin the case for affirmative action by first observing odd distributions among workforce personnel and then jumping immediately from this and no other evidence to conclusions about group-based discrimination. Race and sex discrimination have a well-confirmed history in, for example, the United States. Given this background knowledge, the absence or underrepresentation of women or minority group members in a particular workforce takes on greater significance than it might otherwise have had.[9]

It is reasonable to ask how we should measure underrepresentation. We need some benchmark of a *representative* workforce to use as a standard. In the absence of positive evidence that a particular population group really lacks the capacities to function well in a particular occupation, it is reasonable to start by assuming that any workforce of a reasonable size would show a roughly proportional representation of major population groups to the extent that they are available for employment in the field.

Professor Narveson sometimes claims that affirmative action advocates call simply for proportional representation as such, but that claim is incorrect. Affirmative action goals have generally been tied to statistics about availability in the field in question (and Professor Narveson later acknowledges this). Underrepresentation-given-availability is what functions as a *prima facie* reason to suspect group-based discrimination in a given context. If only 20 percent of all Ph.D.'s in philosophy are female, it is obviously not (in general) appropriate to require that philosophy departments match the half female ratio of the general population.

This sort of reasoning is only a first step in analyzing a workforce. If there is positive evidence in a particular case to show that the minority group members or women who applied for the relevant jobs really were demonstrably less qualified than their nonminority or nonfemale competitors, then no penalty accrues to an employer who fails to meet his or her own preset affirmative action goals. Reverse-preferential affirmative action programs typically call for good record keeping, precisely to allow employers to defend themselves in case they are later "audited" for not having met their affirmative action goals. The possibility of refuting the charge of discrimination in any given case, however, does not diminish the *general* relevance of underrepresentation-given-availability as a benchmark for setting affirmative action goals.

Professor Narveson's second reason for questioning the view that employment practices are significantly race- or sex-biased is that such prejudices would be economically irrational. Race or sex discrimination, in his view, is costly and would simply not interest employers, who always want to hire or promote the best person they can get for the lowest wage they can get away with paying. Whenever women or minority group members really fit such a description, then they would certainly be hired or promoted.

This argument rests on questionable assumptions and flies in the face of incontrovertible historical evidence. For one thing, economic rationality is an ambiguous notion. In the sort of narrow and specifically meaningful sense that would be relevant to employment discrimination, it should refer roughly to the aim of maximizing monetary profits. This notion, however, will not help Professor Narveson make his case, since, depending on the circumstances, race and sex discrimination can be clear money-winners and therefore rational in this sense. A store that caters to a racially prejudiced white clientele, for example, might lose customers if it hires black salespeople.

Professor Narveson notes that Jackie Robinson, the first black major league baseball player, had trouble finding housing when he traveled for road games. Professor Narveson does not, however, tell us how economic rationality by itself solved this problem or opened hotels to blacks in general as paying customers. What finally broke the race barrier in public accommodations nationwide was antidiscrimination law, which, by imposing *penalties* for proven race discrimination in public accommodations, made it economically irrational for hotelowners to turn away black customers.

Few people place monetary profits above all else in their lives. Even in the workplace, most people pursue a diversity of goals. Most people, that is, are not rational merely in the sense of seeking the greatest possible monetary profits but rather in a wider sense of seeking to realize the best possible set that they can of all of what they each value. That notion of rationality, however, weakens Professor Narveson's case even further.

Whenever one's commitments conflict with each other, one must assign priorities and make trade-offs. Some people are racists or misogynists to the core. They might despise certain other groups so fervently that they would rather lose money than have to behave respectfully toward those people. The depth of group-based hostility among human beings is sometimes unfathomable, yet there is, unfortunately, nothing inherently irrational about someone's abiding commitment to it. However despicable he was being, then-governor of Alabama, George Wallace, was not being irrational when he infamously proclaimed, "Segregation today! Segregation tomorrow! Segregation forever!"

Even if people never put racial or other prejudices before monetary profits, their most rational behaviors could still involve unwarranted group-based discrimination for the simple reason that human rationality is exceedingly limited. On modest data bases, we must often make quick decisions. Some of our information is, furthermore, inaccurate. We are, for example, prone to stereotypical thinking about other human beings, especially those who belong to groups with which we have only a distant or hostile acquaintance. We are likely to trust "our own kind," to overvalue their achievements, more than we do others. Mistakenly believing that P-type people are worse than average at J-type jobs, we become predisposed to "seeing" the performance of P-type applicants as inferior. These widespread tendencies no doubt reflect subconscious strategies for decision making under conditions of uncertainty. And evaluating employment candidates is often a highly uncertain process.

Employment candidates usually have to be measured simultaneously according to numerous divergent criteria. Prospective faculty member Jones publishes excellent scholarship but very infrequently; how does she compare to Smith who cranks out three publications a year, of mixed quality? As a teacher, Jones is awkward when leading class discussion but is always available to students outside class; how does her teaching compare to that of Smith who entertains his classes with humor-filled lectures but makes conceptual mistakes and disappears during his official office hours? When multiple and divergent qualities have to be compared, there may often simply be no objective basis for choosing the top candidate. The influence of bias is possible at every step of the way, from the assessment of the minutiae that make up someone's qualifications to the ranking of those minutiae in terms of relative importance. Thus, even the most rational of human assessments is limited both by the finitude of human assessors and by degrees of objective indeterminacy regarding the complex traits being jointly assessed.

Finally, if economic rationality is so effective in eliminating unfair economic discrimination, why then has there existed *so much* unfair economic discrimination? The evidence of race and sex discrimination in U.S. history is incontrovertible. Even if human rationality were superior enough that people would always in the long run come to regard group-based discrimination as a mistake, nevertheless, how long is the "long run" in each case? And why should so many people have to suffer before we get there? More than half a century of professional baseball passed by before the first black man was allowed to play for a major league team. Think of all the worthy black ballplayers who were just born too early. Think of the many more worthy women and minority group members who were just born too early for all the historically discriminatory commonplace occupations that do not require such rare talents.

At this point, we come to a major transition in the debate. Professor Narveson could accept all of my claims about the limitations of rationality and yet still oppose mandated, reverse-preferential affirmative action. This is because he challenges wholesale the right of government to mandate employment practices at all, regardless of whether the employment practices counteracted by those mandates are biased or not. In his view, it is wrong simpliciter for government to intervene in the actions of individuals and associations contrary to the preferences of those agents. He regards such interventions as unjust. An entire conception of justice is at stake in this debate.

Notice that this argument applies to any mandated affirmative action policies, not merely the reverse-preferential sort. Even benign, uncontroversial requirements for wide publication of job announcements could not be mandated if this argument is correct. Indeed, Professor Narveson's arguments apply not just to affirmative action programs, but also to the entire array of antidiscrimination laws. This hidden implication of his views is not highlighted in his essay, but it follows readily from the logic of his arguments.

Notice also, however, that this argument applies *only* to mandated forms of affirmative action. Any affirmative action policy that is voluntarily undertaken by an employer remains at least permissible, even if not obligatory. So long as it is voluntary, it therefore reflects the overall preference calculations of the employer and, hence, should not be hindered. Even conditionally mandated affirmative action, as I suggested earlier, is voluntary in a relevant sense; many companies get along quite well without federal contracts.[10]

That issue aside, the problem of justice looms large. Does justice tell us that unconditionally mandated affirmative action is wrong? According to Professor Narveson's capsule version of it, justice calls for letting people do what they want, so long as their purposes are legitimate.

People should not be arbitrarily forced to "choose against their preferences."

Even as a thumbnail sketch, this concept of justice will not do. A more plausible starting point is the age-old notion of justice as everyone getting her due. This formulation makes it more obvious that the pursuit of my own purposes is constrained by what I owe to others. Even otherwise legitimate preferences might, on grounds of justice, have to give way to overriding moral duties. The debate over affirmative action is a debate over whether or not reverse-preferential affirmative action policies are *legitimate constraints* on the pursuit of economic purposes.

Professor Narveson claims that reverse-preferential affirmative action programs constitute *arbitrary* interferences with individual preferences. The programs are certainly debatable but they are hardly arbitrary. The designated affirmative action categories such as women and blacks reflect the well-documented history of economic exploitation and marginalization of black and female labor in the United States. The affirmative action aim of genuinely reducing workplace discrimination is a reasonable economic goal.

This line of thought takes us to the real heart of the debate. Professor Narveson does not regard discriminatory practices as being wrong in the first place. If they are not wrong, then there is nothing to correct and all substantially nonvoluntary affirmative action policies would indeed be arbitrary interferences with employer preference.

According to this line of reasoning, Professor Narveson's charge that affirmative action calls for hiring "less than the best" is quite irrelevant. So, too, is his claim that affirmative action promotes greater privileges for women and blacks under the guise of equality. These accusations might be flat-out falsehoods and it would not matter one whit. The key premise of Professor Narveson's view is that whoever owns the means of employment may hire whomever they want, however prejudicially they want to do so.

Although Professor Narveson insists that economic rationality will eventually eliminate race or sex bias from the marketplace, nevertheless, that optimistic conviction is no part of his conception of justice as such. In the last analysis, he bases economic entitlement on little more than property rights construed as virtual absolutes. His opposition to affirmative action would still hold firm even if economic rationality were never to make a dent in race or sex prejudice.

For Professor Narveson, whoever owns the means of employment should be able to hire, fire, or promote whomever they want with virtually no governmental regulation. It matters not that the cumulative effects of such decisions might impoverish whole population groups, children included, who are the victims of widespread prejudice. This is the stark reality of Professor Narveson's alternative to conditionally mandated, reverse-preferential affirmative action programs. Surely there is a better way.

More about Feminism[11]

Professor Narveson writes that "the politically correct view about [full-time mothers and homemakers] seems to be to declare them pariahs" and to explain their choice of "domestic pursuits" as the consequence of "still more brainwashing by a sexist society." This brief remark is directed particularly at contemporary feminism. Professor Narveson's statement reveals yet another aspect of the familiar derogatory stereotype of a feminist, an aspect that I previously overlooked. Feminists are sometimes mistakenly thought to be contemptuous of and patronizing toward women who choose the "traditional female role" of full-time homemaker and mother.

This view of feminists is simply false. Although a few feminists, mainly in the late 1960s and early 1970s, made harsh-sounding statements about the social roles of wife, mother, and homemaker, those statements cannot be understood properly out of their original contexts. In context, they were used to make certain critical points about the traditional practices in which women's social roles were embedded. For one thing, as I discussed earlier, feminists have condemned the pervasive male dominance of traditional family life. For another thing, feminists have criticized female socialization practices for overemphasizing domestic activities and underemphasizing other pursuits that might be more suitable to diverse female temperaments and abilities. In addition to these critical lines of thought about domestic traditions, feminists have also worked to abolish the barriers that either kept women from participating in the public world or denied them fair opportunities and rewards for such participation.

Consider the last point first. Because feminists have labored to open up satisfactory opportunities for women in the public world, some audiences might infer that feminists think of the domestic world as inferior by contrast. That, however, would be a fallacious inference. If women had been allowed, say, into the field of carpentry but barred from plumbing, it would not have disparaged carpentry in the least for feminists to have concentrated on arguing that women should be able to be plumbers too.

To fight against the barriers that have kept women out of nontraditional social roles or occupations does not imply any value judgment whatsoever about the roles or occupations that have traditionally been available to women. The point is to open up a multitude of avenues by which women can meet their needs and live satisfying and fulfilling lives. No additional effort is required to get women into mothering and homemaking. Numerous social norms, institutions, practices, and attitudes continue to support women who make these choices. Feminists have concentrated instead on occupations and activities that have traditionally excluded women or for which women have not traditionally received adequate remuneration or recognition.

Second, feminists have challenged the socialization practices that channel girls and women toward mothering and domestic pursuits, regardless of ability or inclination. Professor Narveson accuses feminists of believing that women are "brainwashed by a sexist society." Socialization is not genuinely brainwashing, of course, and no one thinks so. Between brainwashing and utter nondirectedness, however, lies a wide range of possible forms of societal influence. Child rearing for gender roles clearly falls somewhere in between the extremes; it is not usually literal psychological coercion, but it is not a negligible influence either. Much child rearing is still geared toward turning girls into "feminine" women and boys into "masculine" men. Anyone who doubts, for example, that girls much more than boys are prompted toward domestic pursuits should take a stroll through the nearest toy store.[12]

Women are unique individuals, just as are men, and differ among themselves in talents as well as interests. There is no single activity, occupation, or way of life that will satisfy the needs and aspirations of all women, just as there is no single way of life that will do the same for all men. The traditional gender roles of wife and mother are not at all suitable for some women; and, for many more women, are not suitable as full-time occupations. Needs, inclinations, abilities, and even special callings draw different women in different directions. It is precisely the tradition of viewing the wife/mother role (along with the role of sex-partner for men) as primary for women that limits the opportunities for satisfaction in life for *all* women. Diverse women should be able to seek well-being and fulfillment in diverse ways. Feminism is predicated on the insistence that women be no more constrained than are men into choosing one particular way of life or one particular vocation.

Although feminists have led the struggle for diverse opportunities for women, feminists have also championed women's traditional roles—and in rather unique ways. The critics of feminism who charge that feminists disparage traditional homemakers have conveniently overlooked the large feminist literature that vociferously *defends* certain values exemplified by women's traditional activities and practices.

Feminists were the ones who introduced the distinction between working inside the home and working outside the home, to correct the society-wide falsehood that only those mothers who worked at paid employment were really "working mothers." Feminists have long been emphasizing that *every* mother is a working mother.[13] Feminists have thus consistently fought against the cultural devaluation of women's traditional roles and achievements, and fought for women's genuine control over the realm that was supposed to be their own. Feminists, for example, have worked hard to wrest the control of women's reproductive lives away from governments (male-dominated) and churches (male-dominated) and place it in women's own hands. The struggle for abortion rights is well known. Less widely known are the feminist campaigns to make midwifery legal once again, and to bring wonder, meaning, and maternal autonomy back into the birthing experience, reclaiming it, so far as possible, from the impersonal, hi-tech clinical settings to which it had been consigned by the field of modern obstetrics (male-dominated).

In addition, major areas of feminist theory have sought to elevate cultural esteem for the special values that characterize traditional, so-called women's work. Care ethics, a widely influential, cross-disciplinary feminist development, celebrates the nurturance, caring, and general attentiveness to human relationships that characterize women's traditional work in domestic and other intimate interpersonal settings. Many proponents of this view have urged that the socially underappreciated values of caring and nurturance are just as morally worthy, if not more so, than the more typically masculine values of justice and rights toward which social theorists have always disproportionately gravitated.[14] Sara Ruddick's famous feminist publication, *Maternal Thinking*, respectfully explores and honors the intellectual dimensions of women's traditional work in nurturing and rearing children. She extracts from these practices an ethic with international and military significance.[15] These developments typify dominant strains of contemporary feminist thought; they are not the ravings of isolated mavericks.

Another widespread feminist concern about women as homemakers and mothers that has not been given its public due is the feminist concern for welfare mothers and women at the low end of the income scale, for whom full-time homemaking is simply an unaffordable luxury. It is feminism, more than any other research paradigm, that set researchers off investigating the feminization of poverty and the singular hardships facing women who struggle alone to support dependent children. It was feminists who began the campaign for greater legal enforcement of the court-ordered child support that many divorced fathers still routinely evade paying. In general, feminists have worked extensively with others to create a safety net of societal agencies and resources that can help single, divorced, and low-income mothers to care properly for their children and themselves.

Given the high degree of feminist esteem for women's traditional moral concerns and interpersonal skills, and the extensive feminist support for mothers who most need social support networks, it is disturbing to find that critics of feminism portray us as contemptuous toward full-time homemakers and mothers. Why the distortion? Maybe the critics are just naively unfamiliar with feminist writings about mothering and care ethics. In that case, they ought to spend less time criticizing feminism and more time learning about it.

On the other hand, perhaps some critics of feminism are using this misrepresentation as a deliberate subterfuge to take attention away from the real feminist message about traditional families that makes them feel uncomfortable, even threatened. What feminist view could provoke such a response? The answer is easy: the feminist challenge to male domination, in this case, the domination of traditional family life.

Challenging male dominance is the third, and most explosive, of the feminist positions that have provoked the mistaken charge that feminists disparage traditional full-time homemakers. Earlier, I made the obvious point that to criticize male dominance is not to criticize women who live in traditional families. When the critics of feminism accuse us of disparaging homemakers, those critics are changing the subject. The real problem is, and has always been, men's ultimate power over traditional family life, which feminists regard as a moral and material danger for women and children. This point could use some elaboration.

The notion of the traditional family is ambiguous. Heterosexual marriages are traditional in one respect when the husband is the sole income provider and the wife is responsible for the domestic work and primary parenting. A woman who participates in this sort of relationship is not necessarily dominated by her husband. Heterosexual marriages, however, are traditional in a different, and objectionable, respect when husbands make all the major decisions for their family units, exercise ultimate control over the spending of money, and generally hold topmost authority and power in their homes.

In the mildest forms of male dominance, husbands/fathers love and protect their wives and children with wisdom and kindness. Mild male dominance is benevolent paternalism.[16] In the most virulent forms of male dominance, husbands beat up their wives and children and generally tyrannize over their households. Many people will concede that tyrannical husbands are a nasty lot. Despite this concession, however, traditional social practices and institutions have always shamefully tolerated such men.[17] Part of the feminist fight against male family domination has been the uphill struggle to make social institutions more intolerant and punitive toward such abuses as wife-battering, marital rape, and incest. Feminists have also argued that even seemingly *benevolent* male family paternalism is problematic for women in traditional family roles.

A woman who creates a loving and supportive home life for her family members gives them a moral as well as a material gift; such activities can be the source of deep and justified satisfaction for her. Child rearing, even more so, is a domain of breathtaking challenges and transcendent rewards. Child rearing is also a paramount social necessity; when done well, it is a veritable public service. A woman who chooses full-time homemaking and mothering is choosing one of the various honorable vocations now available to women.

There is nothing particularly honorable, however, about the subordination of women to men. There is no reason why a woman who chooses full-time homemaking and mothering should therefore be regarded, or regard herself, as having relinquished to her husband her own autonomous selfhood or an equal share of legitimate control over the home *she makes* or the family *she is raising*. The philosophical tradition is rich with praise for self-determination and the importance of being a ''free man.'' Until the recent decades of contemporary feminist debate, however, the ideals of liberty and autonomy were never applied by conventional (usually male) philosophers to traditional female roles.

To be sure, the concern for self-determination can devolve into a narrow moral obsession that obscures the self-enlarging values of community and interpersonal attachment to others. Nevertheless, substantial self-determination is an important counterbalance to the requirements of endless service and self-sacrifice that threaten to deplete the moral resources of the traditional wife/mother role. At stake is recognition of the legitimacy of women following their own judgments about what is worth valuing and pursuing in the lives they make for themselves and their families. It is no less than a question of women's moral integrity.

Male family dominance threatens more than a woman's moral integrity; it also threatens her own material well-being and that of her children. A woman who is a full-time homemaker and mother in a heterosexual marriage is economically dependent on, and therefore vulnerable to, her husband in a variety of ways.[18] For financial reasons alone, she much more than he needs the marriage to persist. Her financial standard of living would likely plummet after divorce while his would almost certainly rise. Her income-earning husband can thus seriously threaten at any time to leave the marriage as a way of getting what he wants; for her, by contrast, this option is greatly diminished. As a result, she has more need to please and defer to him than vice versa in those inevitable situations in which their desires or values conflict.[19] One overriding concern that keeps many battered women tied to their violent husbands is the fear of losing financial support, a paramount consideration when children are involved.

A woman who chooses life as a full-time homemaker and mother surely does not choose, for its own sake, the subordination and excessive vulnerability that she risks by her financial dependence on her husband. These hazards, however, simply inhere in the nature of financial dependence. Add to that the cultural ideals of masculinity with their incessant pressure on men to be strong, decisive, aggressive, and forceful—and the risk only intensifies.

To be sure, there have always been some women who were strong and independent enough to stand up to their husbands for the views and values to which they were committed. There have also, fortunately, been men who did not avail themselves of the power provided by their breadwinning status and legitimized by masculine ideals. There are, in other words, genuinely good men.[20] Such men, however, run the risk of being regarded as wimps. The comic, but often sympathetic, figure of the "henpecked husband" only makes sense against a background presumption that men ought to prevail in their marriages. "Taming" the "shrew" is part of the Western canon. The rooster-pecked wife, by contrast, is not even a recognized category. Remember that it was *his* castle, after all, the place where he was supposed to be *king*.

It may seem bad manners for feminists to point out these discomforting problems. It would be worse than bad manners, however, to sweep them under an antifeminist carpet. If women are to choose their ways of life with some measure of autonomy and wisdom, then they should be informed about the risks inherent in the available options. In Professor Narveson's words, "we are interested in the truth." The profemale truth about feminism is a crucial part of the story.

Postscript

In his commentary, which follows, Professor Narveson admits that some of my views are reasonable, but minimizes that concession by downplaying the PC import of those views. His approach seems to be this: if it's really PC, then it can't be reasonable; if it's at all reasonable, then it can't be PC. This is a deceptive critical strategy. My arguments support crucial PC innovations (feminism, multiculturalism, affirmative action) and challenge typical PC targets (the Western canon, objectivist pretensions). Where I did not support PC developments outright (speech codes, deconstruction), I nevertheless endorsed some of the concerns underlying them. If my arguments sound too convincing to be politically correct, that might just show that political correctness is more reasonable than the critics would have us believe.

Notes

1. Two cautions seem in order at this point. First, it is worth noticing that Professor Narveson cites very few sources to document his depictions of political correctness or his claims about what is actually going on in academia today.

Second, although I refer collectively in my response essay to multiculturalists, feminists, and so on as "PC advocates" without qualifying the use of this expression, I should point out that the term is not really apt. The expression "political correctness" has acquired an inappropriately derisive connotation in popular debate that is difficult to dispel. Most of those who defend so-called politically correct ideas and policies would not call themselves "PC advocates." I use the term in this discussion only for ease of reference.

2. See Linda Nochlin, "Why Have There Been No Great Women Artists?," in *Women, Art, and Power* (New York: Harper & Row, 1988), pp. 158–63.

3. See Deborah Rhode, *Justice and Gender* (Cambridge, Mass.: Harvard University Press, 1989), pp. 244–53. In many states until recently, a rapist could not be convicted unless the victim's testimony was corroborated by a witness. For a discussion of this issue and the general problem of women's diminished credibility as witnesses in their own rape cases, see Kit Kinports, "Evidence Engendered," *University of Illinois Law Review* 1991, no. 2: 435–40.

4. Obviously, the relevant categories can overlap and someone can belong to more than one of them.

5. By refusing to take federal moneys, colleges and universities can analogously avoid the conditional congressional mandate to implement affirmative action in educational programs.

6. Professor Narveson brings out some of the problems with the compensa-

tion defense. For a complex discussion of the various arguments, see Bernard Boxhill, *Blacks and Social Justice* (Totowa, N. J.: Rowman & Allanheld, 1984), chap. 7.

7. Many studies provide evidence of male bias, while many others do not. Several recent meta-analyses (which analyze large bodies of existing research data comprehensively) suggest an overall absence of significant bias against women. Those meta-analyses, however, do not take adequate account of the wide variations in the research data they analyze. A. H. Eagly and A. Mladinic argue, in a forthcoming meta-analysis, that the research data do support the claim that gender bias occurs under certain conditions, for example, when either the performance domain or the behavior being evaluated are traditionally masculine or when the evaluator is male. These particular features are highly relevant to affirmative action employment contexts. See Eagly and Mladinic's "Are People Prejudiced against Women?: Some Answers from Research on Attitudes, Gender Stereotypes, and Judgments of Competence," *The European Review of Social Psychology*, ed. W. Stroebe and M. Hewstone (New York: Wiley, forthcoming 1994).

8. Kurt Kraiger and J. Kevin Ford, "A Meta-analysis of Ratee Race Effects in Performance Ratings," *Journal of Applied Psychology* 70, no. 1 (1985): 60. The authors give good reasons for thinking that the lower performance evaluations received by blacks from white "raters" is at least partly due to rater bias, and that actual performance differences between black and white ratees provide no more than part of the explanation (pp. 61–62). Note that this is a meta-analysis, involving a comprehensive survey of research results (to that time) on this topic.

9. Such statistical assessments only make sense, of course, in cases in which the workforce is large enough for statistical distributions to be significant. Small employers and occupations with small numbers of people are not amenable to this sort of analysis; it is not that discrimination cannot be shown in such cases, but rather that it will have to be shown on different grounds. Small employers, however, have, from the outset, been exempt from antidiscrimination law.

10. We should note that in the United States, enforcement of affirmative action has had a sporadic history, ceasing altogether under the Reagan and Bush administrations. Although enforcement has resumed under the Clinton administration, it is still very likely that any reverse-preferential affirmative action practiced in the United States right now is largely voluntary.

11. Scholars familiar with and sympathetic toward feminist literature will probably find this section to be old hat. There is, for example, no discussion here of the most recent feminist controversies such as that of race differences among women. My selective focus was prompted mainly by Professor Narveson's emphatic e-mail correspondence on the particular topic addressed here, an emphasis that, I believe, reflects yet another widespread misunderstanding of feminism that needs to be addressed.

12. A great deal of contemporary girlhood socialization is oriented toward glamour and vanity pursuits, with ''Barbie'' shamelessly touted as the leading ''role model.'' The adult hyperemphasis on the prettiness of female (but not male) children begins when babies are newborns; a stroll through the nearest infant/toddler clothing store makes that differentiation clear. The socialization of females toward prettiness and vanity connects indirectly with their socialization toward domestic pursuits. Fussing over their looks is a key way for women to attract male sexual attention and, eventually, male marital interest.

13. The early second-wave feminists who called attention to the real work carried out by women as mothers and housewives were often Marxist-feminists who were especially concerned to show that women's work counted as genuine production even if it was not part of the system of wage labor and commodity exchange. See, for example, Margaret Benston, ''The Political Economy of Women's Liberation,'' *Feminist Frameworks: Alternative Theoretical Accounts of the Relations between Women and Men*, 2nd. ed., ed. Alison M. Jaggar and Paula S. Rothenberg (New York: McGraw-Hill, 1984), pp. 239–47. Reprinted from *Monthly Review*, September 1969: 13–25. See also Natalie J. Sokoloff, ''Motherwork and Working Mothers,'' *Feminist Frameworks*, pp. 259–66. Adapted from Natalie J. Sokoloff, *Between Money and Love: The Dialectics of Women's Home and Market Work* (A Praeger Special Studies, 1980).

14. Feminists have debated the apparent association between different moral perspectives and gender; see, for example, the various essays in Mary Jeanne Larrabee, ed., *An Ethic of Care* (New York: Routledge, 1993). My goal here is not to take sides on this issue but rather simply to point out that many feminists applaud the moral concerns widely associated with traditionally female social roles.

15. Sara Ruddick, *Maternal Thinking: Towards a Politics of Peace* (New York: Ballantine Books, 1989).

16. It is curious that philosophers who ''go ballistic'' over the thought of paternalism by governments or between co-equal citizens should be so unconcerned about the widespread paternalism of husbands toward wives in traditional marriages.

17. See, for example, Dorie Klein, ''The Dark Side of Marriage: Battered Wives and the Domination of Women,'' in *Judge, Lawyer, Victim, Thief: Women, Gender Roles, and Criminal Justice*, ed. Nicole Hahn Rafter and Elizabeth Anne Stanko (Boston: Northeastern University Press, 1982), pp. 83–107.

18. This discussion is based on Susan Moller Okin's well-documented study, *Justice, Gender, and the Family* (New York: Basic Books, 1989), especially chap. 7, ''Vulnerability by Marriage.''

19. Anyone who really thinks that this is an overly adversarial view of marriage and that marriage is a blissful harmony of two concordant hearts, minds, and wills has not been married for any length of time, and has certainly not raised children with a spouse.

20. Said in memory of my father, whose ways of goodness I grow to appreciate more and more with time.

Response

Jan Narveson

At the outset, Professor Friedman mentions several recent developments in academic life that form the background of our inquiry: critics on what she terms "the left" propose what she considers "reforms" that will "revamp a host of traditional academic practices and attitudes," and it is those allegedly traditional practices, she suggests, to which the "correctness" label should really be attached. The aforesaid "left" wishes to accuse American education in particular, and much else about contemporary life in general, of "European, American, heterosexual, and masculine biases that continue to permeate traditional research and pedagogy." And they tell us of "new research paradigms emphasizing race, gender, ethnicity, and sexual orientation as analytical categories." A plethora of issues are thus raised, most of which cannot be discussed in detail. My response, however, certainly gives no credence to traditions simply as such—I have, indeed, no use whatever for the categories of "left" and "right": both parties, as she describes them, are merely different kinds of illiberal thinkers, in my book. I instead try to identify the supposedly traditional practice, suggest a possible rationale for it, and then ask what the basis of the purportedly "radical" critique, in each case, might be. For example, my essay points out that in the humanities, there simply is no subject unless the notion of aesthetic or literary value makes sense and has some application. Perhaps it doesn't, after all. But that wouldn't help the erstwhile "reformer"; *substituting* ideas of cultural multiplicity for the evaluative concepts in question makes nonsense of the humanities, and therefore no recognizable "reform" along the proposed lines would be possible, even if reform were in order. The right way to do these things is to look for such values wherever one finds them, rather than to accuse those who differ of seeing reality through some kind of political bias. Thus, for instance, I

133

(an American/Canadian) attribute the predominance of Greeks, Germans, and British in anthologies of philosophical classics to the fact that they, on any reasonable showing, are the greatest philosophers up until very recently. No self-respecting Canadian philosopher would put any Canadians on such a list; scarcely any American would go beyond suggesting Peirce for marginal inclusion. This is "bias" at work? How? Bias against women? Well, prior to the present, when there are many fine woman philosophers, what in truth is there? Very little, and that rather unimpressive by the standards of Kant, Plato, Descartes—and that in full recognition of various biases of which they may be more or less plausibly accused. Warts and all, Kant is a great philosopher, whether the reader be American, German, or Chinese. Jane Austen is a great novelist by any reasonable standard, not because she is a female and "represents women," but because she is brilliant, charming, masterful in her portrayal of character, and so on; on the other hand, no woman composer of the nineteenth (or any) century compares with her—there are, as yet, no musical or philosophical Jane Austens. There are, however, several men, and anybody who knows anything about music can reel off their names with alacrity. Biases can happen, certainly: but that they "permeate" the research and pedagogy of recent times is, I think, just false, and indeed, itself a judgment that would only be supported by bias—especially, at the present time, political bias, buttressed by a generous measure of sheer ignorance.

Thus we come to the subject of political bias. A considerable part of my effort in this exchange has been devoted to reminding us that the word "political" does have a quite specific meaning. We have politics insofar as we have government, especially in the central case of the government of a community or nation, but also, analogously, with the government of, say, the university. Governments call the shots, lay down and enforce the law, and, in short, exert more or less coercive power over the community.

Bias, in turn, involves conflicting aims. To say that someone is biased is to say that she has some purpose, aim, or project, identified as the central one in the context, and that some irrelevant interest, urge, or desire induces that agent to decide some question on the basis of it instead of on the basis of that central one. *Political* bias, then, is bias which affects governmental policies and practices. All use of the powers of government requires people to do things they have no desire to do, or forbids them to do what they have an interest in doing. Bias in the exercise of those powers is necessarily wrong, for it means imposing costs on people that are not justified by the proper purposes of government.

A view about those purposes does certainly inform my essay and, I presume, is broadly shared by Professor Friedman as well, I hope, as virtually all of our readers. On this view, government exists and is justified—if it ever is—solely to promote the common good of those governed; and that "good" is the good as seen and accepted *by* the governed themselves. That is the liberal view of government. According to it, government exists to serve *us*, not vice-versa.

In individual cases, however, direction of one's effort toward the good of some particular people, such as oneself and one's friends or family, while you may want to call that "bias," is not political, though it may have a moral aspect. It is not the purpose of individuals to promote the common good, though most of us hope to do so in our small ways. Our purposes are typically nonuniversal, then, and so, if "biased" meant "motivated by a concern for some rather than others," virtually all human actions would have to be said to be "biased." But that would be a silly and irrelevant, indeed a wildly biased, use of the term "bias."

In order to apply the concept of bias, we must decide which are the central or normatively primary interests of the agent whose bias or lack of it is in question, before the concept of bias is even applicable. Unless I am interested in the truth, a tendency to decide instead on the basis of some other interests of mine is not "bias." When I sit down to breakfast, my interest in satisfying my own hunger and enjoying the food before me is essentially irrelevant to the promotion of human knowledge. There is no question of "bias" in my manipulating my fork in one way rather than another merely because in so doing I fail to advance the theory of differential equations one whit.

If we have rightly identified what matters more, then to act out of bias is to act from some motive that prompts a different line of action to the central one for the context; moreover, to call it "bias" is to imply that that line of action is to some degree at cross purposes with the central one. Bias, then, is inherently counterproductive. That's what makes it a vice rather than a virtue. Thus I have argued that genuinely discriminatory business practices, in light of the central interest of maximizing profits, are necessarily costly; hiring on the basis of sex instead of scholarly capability reduces scholarly output; selecting texts on the basis of their "representativeness" of some particular culture or group instead of their intrinsic interest and appeal is, in the context of a literary course as such, biased—though it would not be so at all were the course intended to study the variety of human cultures. And so on.

Who or what determines what is central? Where only one's own affairs are in question, the answer is that one must do this oneself. There exist, for example, some genuine racists, people who somehow suppose that they have a major interest in dealing only with persons of race R, and in branding all others "inferior" or sub-human. This will cost them a lot in the way of other values—in the case of the Nazis, it deprived Germany of the services of several million Jews, including a large percentage of all the creative geniuses of the time. Still, if they insist on holding other values, such as getting rich or acquiring knowledge, to be of lesser importance, then so be it. To speak of Nazi "bias" against Jews—besides absurdly understating the case—is to imply that the Nazis had other purposes more important than anti-Semitism. Given the intellectual poverty of Nazidom, one might well deny that—their "thinkers" were two-bit twerps; but in any case, whatever may be said of personal Nazi values, if there really were any such, those values were pursued almost entirely by the wholly illegitimate means of marshalling state power on their behalf.

But most of those whose actions we are concerned with in these essays are not acting as individuals dealing only with their own affairs. Whom I marry is my business, but whom I hire on behalf of the Philosophy Department, or how I spend the public's involuntarily extracted money, is not. Once married, however, one takes on obligations, and having, as it were, married the academy, my actions qua academic are likewise not merely "my business." My connections to others in this endeavor create responsibilities and duties. So academic freedom, for example, is not the freedom to goof off in the classroom, though it is the freedom to judge that Thomas Hobbes is one of the greatest of all moral and political philosophers—and for Professor Friedman to make the opposite judgment. We are free to make such judgments, but not to have them be right simply *by* making them; on the contrary, in making them we submit our views to the judgment of impartial reason from whatever quarter, and must defend them in the appropriate places.

I have not, on the other hand, "married" my country—either the one I was born in (the U.S.) or the one I have lived in for many years (Canada). Governments do have a purpose: namely, to promote the common good of their citizens. Now, we doubtless do owe our fellows, including our fellow citizens, something, but we do not owe the government, as such, anything at all. De facto governments of the day have their opinions, as may be, and I have mine: either of us may be wrong, but certainly the government has, to put it mildly, no monopoly on the truth—including the truth about what it ought to be doing—even if it has a monopoly on the police power. It is an important matter, then, when government policies appear to be guilty of bias, and another kind of important matter when universities do. In both cases, there is a betrayal of an important trust. But in the case of government, which no one can escape, the betrayal is fundamental and constitutes injustice. In the case of universities, it may do so too, though at least in their case "divorce" is possible if all else fails—universities are easily "escaped" and indeed, most people manage to avoid them readily enough. In the meantime, though, they can be guilty of misleading their clientele—those who seek education—in any number of ways, and in the process ill-serving the public, which they do presume to be serving. Prominent among the potential kinds of failure would be its embracing of policies not on the basis of their likelihood of promoting their purported objectives, but instead of securing essentially nonacademic goals, such as sexual or racial "equality." Universities must relevantly distinguish among the more and less competent—between those who contribute more and those who contribute less to human knowledge by way of teaching and research. The possibility of promoting human knowledge, by either or both of those means, is predicated on the assumption that knowledge is *real*, that is, that when we know, what we know about exists independently of our imaginations or desires, that its existence is in principle publicly knowable, and thus that there can be genuine criteria of acceptability on the basis of which diverse persons can evaluate rival claims to the status of knowledge. Theories purporting to show that there simply can't be any such claims at all imply that academia is a mistake and universities should close down. Such views would undermine the applicability of any notion of "bias." Of course, the inserted qualification, "if true," as Professor Friedman agrees, is the catch: to show that the condition is met would automatically be to refute the claim being asserted—an anomaly we shall leave committed deconstructionists to ponder.

Meanwhile, if we suppose that there is knowledge to be had and that we have reasonable confidence that some forays after it have better prospects of success than others, then we are also in a position to identify bias. Racial, sexual, and the innumerable other biases not mentioned by Professor Friedman are always possible, and frequently enough actual. These are always to be deplored and sometimes to be countered by authoritative means. However, a very large question now arises about the appropriate criteria for identifying them. The tendency nowadays, ubiquitous in all of the areas we are considering under the heading of political correctness, is to take the existence of statistical disparities in, say, academic performance by different groups in particular fields as itself sufficient evidence of the existence of bias somewhere along the line, and as constituting at least *prima facie* reason to take action to "correct" the disparities in question. It is not, I hasten to add, clear whether Professor Friedman subscribes to this idea in any of its versions, and if not, that is very much to the good. But it is clear that much of the policy we are discussing appears to be predicated on it, and certainly it is important to expose it for the fallacy it is.

For that way lies madness. There is quite obviously no *logical* connection between virtually all contexts of "performance" in virtually all human endeavours and such factors as race or sex or any of the countless other variables that are likewise logically independent of performance; this is conspicuously so in the case of academia. This very condition is logically required to apply any notion of bias. If sex is literally relevant to performance criteria, then hiring on the basis of sex is not biased: models for *Ebony* magazine, selection of "top Jewish intellectual, 1992," "best dressed man," and a few others obviously make race and sex necessary conditions of eligibility for the distinctions in question, and when they do, there is no call for describing the selection as "biased" or in the current sense "discriminatory." But such factors are almost always not relevant. And when they are not, then the fact that eighty-five percent of those who do well in the area are female, or male, or black, or left-handed, or short, or red-haired, or descended from Hungarians, or whatever, does not on the face of it prove that any kind of bias was exercised in the process of identifying the high-performers. They may merely show that such people happen to be exceptionally talented at that particular endeavour, or more highly motivated; any number of possible explanations may apply, if explanation is sought.

Bias by individuals acting on their own behalf may warp judgment, prompting the agent to perform irrational actions, actions that run contrary to one's main purposes. But such bias involves no fundamental injustice in the more narrowly political and moral senses of that term. That is reserved for cases where we impose costs on others, not for ones where we impose costs on ourselves while doing less good for others than we might.

Now, literary, musical, and visual values all relate in some way to culture, to be sure: but not by being a product of some sort of conspiracy for political power. That these values are logically independent of things like sex, race, and even culture is and has always been obvious. But it does not follow, for example, that the literary and artistic products of different sexes and races must necessarily be equally important or equally valuable qua literary and artistic, though they may be important qua example, as illustrating interesting human capacities from other points of view.

Those who want to assail the very notion of value have one set of tubes to take us down. As I say, if there is no such thing as aesthetic value, then art makes no sense, and culture, insofar as it is concerned with the production of the aesthetically interesting, is absurd. Now, it is not clear how many proponents of politically correct policies are serious about the attack on aesthetic value as a general category, and Professor Friedman is not among them. But others wish to attack on a narrower and more promising front. They dissent from a wide array of value judgments familiar in "our" culture (though hardly unique to it): that Beethoven is a great composer or Shakespeare a great playwright, say. These other critics of "the left," if they accept that there are values to be experienced, perceived, and enjoyed, need to give us some sort of plausible aesthetic reasons for reversing these familiar and, I would say, enormously plausible judgments. But in fact we don't get them; instead, we just get tired claims about racism and sexism, factors which no doubt were present in various classical writers, but to which nothing like the proposed degree of importance can plausibly be attached. Is one who can put into the mouths of his heroines the lines of a Portia or a Cleopatra to be tarred with the brush of "sexism"? That looms as a pretty paltry criticism when weighed against the power of the lines in question. (There can be more difficult cases. Consider Leni Riefenstahl—herself a pretty significant counterexample against any general thesis that women have been excluded in the arts. The actual evils of the regime her films were made to extol does really tell against the aesthetic value of her cinematic endeavor. In the case of propaganda, the aesthetic necessarily merges with the moral and political. Yet even in this case, we can appreciate the greatness of many aspects of her art, even while deploring its ostensible purpose.)

But meanwhile, as I say, we do not actually get anything else from the left in the way of support for the criticisms in question—unless, that is, you count grand philosophical assertions of the inherent equality of all in all respects as "something" along this line. In this regard, I suggest that postmodern literary criticism and its attendant pseudo-philosophy are, in the end, sophomoric bores rather than significant contributions to the criticism of art and life.

Here, though, enters Professor Friedman who, if I understand her, has likewise not much sympathy for the conceptual syndromes to which I have alluded. I do, though, have difficulty identifying just which recognizably politically correct positions she does wish to affirm. Her first subject is speech codes, and here a certain divergence of aim between us is perhaps discernible. My question about speech codes is whether we should empower authorities to forcibly prevent people from speaking to others who are willing to hear; whether, indeed, we should not instead forcibly intervene, if need be, to eject or punish those who would do that. I am interested, in short, in the *right* to speech. This is quite compatible with deploring many sorts of speech, including those she lists. But should the police descend on those who call me names I dislike? I think not; and, it seems, neither does she.

On the other hand, those subjected to insult must have some recourse, and if the insult takes place in a public venue, it is in general clear that all ought to keep civil tongues in their heads; and that is clearer still in, say, the lecture hall or the classroom. But the imposition of codes, especially of the type that political correctness represents, is not generally the way to do this. There are any number of ways of insulting, verbally intimidating, harassing, needling, or wounding. If you put a tiny subset of these on a list—hate speech, for instance—and make those who utter those liable to be ejected from the university, the question, ''Why those ways and not others?'' becomes unanswerable; at the same time, any attempt to ''ban'' them all is intolerable and uninterpretable. On this, she and I are not far apart, I gather.

I will take this opportunity to emphasize a distinction between two different reasons in support of freedom of speech, not, I guess, sufficiently emphasized in my essay. One reason stems from the interest in promoting human knowledge, which I take to be the general purpose of institutions of higher education. In this context, those who monopolize discussion time in the classroom on behalf of irrelevant, exploded, or demonstrably silly theories, for example, may be silenced by lecturers interested in getting on with the subject. But people who natter peacefully to each other over the back fence, contributing nothing whatever to human knowledge, may not be suppressed on any such grounds, regardless of that noncontribution. Society is not a classroom, and many speech activities are not particularly concerned with knowledge-promotion. The right to speak nonetheless is assured instead by the general freedom of the individual to do what he or she wishes, so long as the freedom of others is not thereby impugned. The trouble with speech codes is not that they prevent the promotion of knowledge, as such; it is that they enable authorities to exercise arbitrary powers over individuals: powers to impose relatively draconian penalties for relatively trivial wrongs or, in most cases, activities that simply aren't on any reasonable showing wrong at all.

Nor do we differ widely, I believe, on the so-called Western canon, insofar as there is such a thing.. As the reader now knows, I do not defend the existence of canons on the ground that they are necessary for some such vague end as the maintenance of Western political institutions. For one thing, they surely aren't, in any clear sense; but in any case, that is not the right defense. The right defense of "canons" is that those who are interested in the kinds of literatures of which the canonical items are examples have found those items to be especially interesting, stimulating, insightful, beautiful, seminal, and so on, and thus it is to be hoped that interested students will likewise find them so. In any case, if our purpose is to get a handle on the field, then acquainting ourselves with its seminal, important, or great examplars is surely sensible. Those who insist on regarding every novel of Austen or Dickens or even Hemingway as a political tract of some kind are simply missing the point. But the very idea of a canon implies that there is some reality, some intersubjective plausibility, to a wide array of literary and artistic judgments, and accordingly to the possibility that other works outside the canon are likely to be worth reading as well. The canon is a pedagogical device; and I pointed out that it is surely good pedagogy to read some of the indifferent or downright bad along with the good and the great. But it is not good pedagogy or good anything to read works from other cultures simply because they have a "right to be read," say, or because their creators are, after all, fellow human beings just like oneself; nor to insist that a curriculum must be devoted in some proportion—say, equal proportions—to writers from other cultures, or other anythings.

Now, Professor Friedman does not in fact call for anything so relatively precise. She thinks that more diversity is a good thing—which is, no doubt, sometimes a safe enough conjecture. And she probably does so for the good reasons I suggested: that they might be interesting, and that in any case we need to understand other people in today's small world, especially when they live right down the street. Still, we do get some suggestion from her of the political correctness view as I have discussed it: the "relevant voices," she says, must "adequately represent the variety of all human viewpoints: female no less than male, black no less than white, poor no less than rich." Well, *why*? For what supposed purposes "represent"? "Viewpoints" on *what?* And what does she mean by "no less than"? Van Gogh's depiction of "The Potato Eaters," say, will serve very well for the purpose: he no doubt "represents" the poor in this famous painting. Indeed, he depicts them, and in so doing tells more about them, very likely, not only than the

proverbial thousand words but probably several musty volumes. Still, it
is he, a genius, who does the depicting, and not they themselves. And
what *makes* him a genius is his ability to depict this and other things—
though mostly, one might note, things with no political significance:
sunflowers, night skies, furniture. What makes his work important is
that, and not that he is some kind of political representative, bringing to
us the vote of some segment of suffering humanity. (Whom might he
politically represent—the "emotionally challenged," maybe?) There's
no telling who next will be able to do for us what a Van Gogh does: but
then, that is exactly why we should *not* insist on having x percent females, y percent gays, w percent Seventh-Day Adventists, z percent
left-handeds, and so on, cluttering up the walls of our museums or our
selections of presumptively worthwhile authors. Let us have among our
authors those who write well, indeed magnificently, or who have much
to say that is worth listening to. The sheer fact that the author belongs
to class X or Y, as defined by criteria independent of literary merit,
counts for nothing, insofar as our purposes are literary.

That said, Professor Friedman admirably points to one of the main
features of the specifically Western canon that is, in intellectual matters,
its pride, and that perhaps above all: namely, that of encouraging and
manifesting critical reflection and indeed, self-criticism, and along with
it openness to the views, or more generally the expressions, including
the literatures, of others. Surely the Roger Kimballs and the Alan
Blooms do not dissent from those virtues, and if they think that Western
civilization depends on the retaining of a "canon," this is likely because what is most valuable in Western civilization largely consists of
values such as those. But as to connecting canons with "national interests," that is a boat I have no interest in clambering into.

It seems to me, then, that the substance of what Professor Friedman
defends is modestly defensible, but is not obviously "political correctness." That, I think, is much more nearly what I have attacked in my
essay: the insistence on the "representations" of all cultures, and so
on, as a matter of *right*, the rejection of literary or artistic evaluation as
cloaks for Western interests, and the like. I applaud that she appears to
be on my side, but remind the reader that there are real people out there
who maintain the sinister and absurd views I attempted to expose in my
essay. More importantly, there are people out there who impose policies
that would only make sense if they did hold approximately those ab-
surdities. They are philosophical ideas—and bad ones.

Turning next to the subject of truth, there is a major need to make a
philosophical distinction between two inquiries: (a) the extremely narrow, though very interesting, subject of truth in the sense of the attempt

to analyze the notion or concept; and (b) the very much broader subjects of why truth should be thought valuable, how one is to go about arriving at it, and what sort of human proclivities might either promote or detract from success in its pursuit in any given area. The former inquiry asks, what does it mean to say that p is true? To answer that, we need to articulate the concept of truth-bearers: what is it that is true—sentences, statements, propositions, ideas? And then we need to clarify whether truth is literally a relation between such things and the reality they purport to be about, or something else; and so on. Some of the postmoderns evidently suppose themselves to be discussing this narrow subject—though one hopes not, and there is room to doubt it.

The second is quite another matter. It is in that arena that we hear of such things as ''feminist standpoint theory,'' and a ''notion of objectivity that does not aim to be value-free,'' and so on. In short essays such as these, one cannot expect Professor Friedman to explain much about such notions, but there is at least a looming dilemma for those wishing to elevate feminism to any epistemologically fundamental status. Do they mean that there are truths that cannot be understood except by women? If so, it must follow that we males are incapable of understanding what women—or at least those women—are talking about. That means that their discourse must be indistinguishable from nonsense so far as males are concerned. And that offers precious little prospect of persuading us. On the other hand, if we *can* understand it, then where is the basicness of this supposed standpoint? People do talk of feminine intuition; but we do not suppose that *what* those who have it are said to be intuiting is intrinsically incommunicable except as one woman to another, and we certainly don't suppose it should or can be elevated to the status of science.

Which brings up the question of what those who profess to ''question'' the idea of ''objective truth'' could possibly suppose themselves to be doing. What is the corresponding idea of subjective truth supposed to be? Truth about subjects? Very well. But are claims about subjects necessarily subjective? Why? Why suppose that whether a given person, a given subject, actually does have the property attributed to him or her in the statements in question is itself a matter about which are no facts to be known? If so, what happened to the supposed ''truth'' whose allegedly subjective status is being touted?

But in fact, Professor Friedman does think that the questions about our society raised in this volume are amenable to pretty straightforward empirical investigation. I applaud. But insofar as these are brought to bear on practical issues, facts are of course not enough. We must have a good normative theory as well. In that respect she is less forthcoming. The underlying theory I have attributed to political correctness is that of a generalized egalitarianism. That idea, I believe, makes no sense; but neither is there very much to be said for any partial egalitarianism, until we get to the most fundamental principles of morals, which, I hold, are necessarily the same for all. Indeed, it is precisely the violation of those principles, specifically their impact on human freedom, that is objectionable about egalitarianisms of these kinds. We do not, however, hear from Professor Friedman what she proposes instead, and this makes it rather hard to respond to her views, for her many detailed and piecemeal claims do not point, so far as I can see, clearly in any one overall direction.

This brings us to her views on feminism. One problem in discussing that collection of views is that it is such a diverse collection that she might have done well to note, in her reference to "widespread feminist-bashing," the rather considerable amount of bashing that some groups of feminists inflict on others, by way of adding perspective. Still, she presumably does identify a general theme on which (almost?) all feminists would agree when she speaks of the "exploitation, abuse, and oppression of women," which she evidently holds to be widespread in our society. Many feminists maintain that ours is a male-dominated, "patriarchal" society, and she seems to have some sympathy with that view. There are two questions: first, whether the tag fits the facts, which is very debatable indeed nowadays; and second, what if anything should be done about it at the level of policy or morals.

There are many phenomena here and likely they do not all call for the same conceptual treatment. Wife-battering, for example, does happen (as does husband-battering, though it doesn't get equal billing). This abhorrent practice may well thrive in part because of inadequate social disapproval and an attitude that if it's domestic, then outsiders are not to interfere, no matter how outrageous the behavior may be. The outrage ought to be there, indeed. But what can a philosopher do besides concur in the outrage? Doubtless this is primarily a psychological, not a philosophical, matter: batterers are bullies, and bullies are generally cowards, people with inadequate senses of self-worth, which impels them to the contemptible habit of taking their inadequacies out on the weak. Whatever the reason, it obviously fails on the score of justice. The strong may be admired in weight-lifting competitions or when hauling heavy boxes upstairs, but not when assaulting people—their wives or anyone else. There is surely no room for interesting *philosophical* disagreement about such things.

But there may be when it comes to what sort of things to do about it. For example, we might redefine the notion of abuse in such a way that it is virtually impossible to tell whether one is abusing someone or not ("He made my eardrums vibrate!"), thus greatly expanding the set of abusers at the stroke of a pen. Or we could abolish intimacy altogether, Antioch-style. But instead of throwing out babies with bathwater, surely the main need is to try to bring it about that spouse-abusers lose rather than gain from their abuse, perhaps by making them subject to similar treatment and by having them pay all the medical bills. Such things will help. More than the sum of any other measures that can be taken, though, is to bring up children properly in the first place, in homes with ample love and freedom, reasonable discipline, and stability. But presumably we are in no disagreement about that, either.

Which brings us to the one major matter on which, I take it, we are in at least some disagreement: affirmative action. Here there is a need to emphasize further a distinction not made much of in my treatment: between compulsory programs, dictated by governments, and genuinely voluntary programs, if there be any such, dictated by the sentiment or the as-may-be "philosophy" of privately acting institutions engaging in it. My discussion took the first sort as central; *inter alia*, it implies that private organizations would have the right to engage in such programs if they chose. As indeed they may—though, as my opening discussion argues, any such programs are likely to be at the cost of the organization's primary goals, whatever they may be: profit, knowledge, the propagation of their particular religious faith, and so on; and since those are the goals on behalf of which employees in such endeavors take themselves to be working, employing new ones on irrelevant grounds runs at least a danger of letting down those already on hand. Those programs are for such purposes unwise, but not necessarily *wrong*, depending on how those institutions are related to their employees. For one may, after all, wrong one's employees by instituting counterproductive policies, of which affirmative action is a prime example.

Contemporary academics in North America are, I would say, almost professionally biased against the free market. When I point out that discrimination is inherently counterproductive from the point of view of the practitioner, they counter with charges that in an environment where discrimination is practiced elsewhere, the enterprise may capitalize on it. And this is certainly true, as illustrated by the scramble for lucrative government contracts by private firms. Everyone prefers a free lunch, or one at reduced price where someone else, such as the hapless taxpayer, bears the burden. But while this is no surprise, it hardly shows that there is anything wrong with the free enterprise system. It shows, rather, that there is something wrong with coercive programs—which is my point. They are also the wrong ways to "combat" alleged discrimination. Genuinely discriminatory practices are unlikely to be sustained except by force, and the thing to do is dismantle the force that sustains it, rather than trying to impose nondiscrimination by counterforce of law. (See, for example, Thomas Sowell's instructive example of southern bus systems, which were segregated by town council enactments, not by the private companies that owned them originally.[1])

But our central interest here as philosophers is in the conceptual foundations of such programs. The question is whether there are good arguments for them; and my answer is that, in general, there are not. Such programs are predicated on the principle that the fact that a set of people were badly treated in the past is somehow supposed to constitute reason in itself to impose counter-preferential treatment on the *class* from which their erstwhile oppressors were drawn. In the present case—affirmative action in academia on behalf of women—statistical analysis shows that the alleged pattern of discrimination against women does not hold anyway; but be that as it may, a program that punishes current nonoppressors in order to benefit individuals who are not themselves victims of the alleged oppression is an absurdity, especially when offered in the name of justice. And the absurdity is much compounded when one observes the devastating effects it visits on the academic community.

Some readers may be inclined to sneer at the idea that there are such effects. But when a highly qualified male is passed over in favor of a female who is not only less qualified on the face of it, but not even in the field advertised for, all in the name of a policy of "fairness" to women, it is difficult to see what room for genuine argument there is. (That there isn't is perhaps attested to by the fact that in defense of the practice one rarely sees anything but repetition, combined with more sneering.) But the example just mentioned is not rare or isolated nowadays: it is virtually typical, and done not only with the blessing but often enough at the instigation of higher university authorities.

In the question-begging ideological atmosphere of the present day, supporters will proceed to urge that those fields passed over were the "wrong" ones anyway: the institution in question *should* be offering more in the way of field X, which happens to be the field of specialization of the woman in question, rather than Y, which the department concerned judges to be needed for its academic program. Or it should be acting as a role model, even though under the auspices of the allegedly repressively masculine regime of former times, the number of women motivated to complete Ph.D.'s increased dramatically in all fields. It seems that anything will do by way of a reason to avoid the obvious objection to a practice which calls for hiring on the basis of irrelevant attributes. But what is especially galling is that those defending such practices do so in the name of equity or fairness themselves.

I also emphasized that the supposed beneficiaries of such programs inherit a special problem, in that their colleagues will inevitably perceive them as occupying their positions on the basis of something other than merit—since, after all, that is exactly why they *are* there. In this respect, indeed, Professor Friedman would do well to denounce affirmative action as applied to women as one more masculine plot, designed to ensure that such men as do occupy positions in the fields where it is employed will in time be surrounded by female mediocrities by comparison with whom they will look (because they probably are) outstanding. Neither this nor the practice itself is such as to promote harmony and productiveness in a working community.

My main points, then, are, first, that what is normally called discrimination is an essentially irrational practice in itself, making it puzzling that people should suppose it to be a widespread phenomenon in need of major legal combatting; second, that the existence of statistical discrepancies between the employment of one group rather than another in a given area is not in itself evidence of "discrimination," so that the familiar practice of calling for laws to enforce equalization is not justified and not just; and finally, that programs of affirmative action inherently punish the innocent while ensuring discord where they are practiced.

Notes

1. Thomas Sowell, *Preferential Policies* (New York: Morrow, 1990). See especially pp. 20–24. A further insightful section on employment discrimination follows, pp. 25–31.

Index

About the Authors

Marilyn Friedman, associate professor of philosophy at Washington University in St. Louis, is the author of *What Are Friends For?: Feminist Perspectives on Personal Relationships and Moral Theory* (Cornell University Press), the coeditor of *Feminism and Community* (Temple University Press, forthcoming), and coeditor of *Mind and Morals: Essays on Ethics and Cognitive Science* (Bradford/MIT, forthcoming). Her essays have appeared in the *Journal of Philosophy*, *Ethics*, *Hypatia*, and elsewhere. She has directed a women's studies program and edited the newsletter of the (U.S.) Society for Women in Philosophy.

Jan Narveson, professor of philosophy at the University of Waterloo in Ontario, Canada, is the author of more than one hundred papers in philosophical periodicals and of three books: *Morality and Utility* (Johns Hopkins), *The Libertarian Idea* (Temple University Press), and *Moral Matters* (Broadview). He is the editor of *Moral Issues* (Oxford University Press). Professor Narveson is on the editorial boards of a dozen journals, is a Fellow of the Royal Society of Canada, and sits on its Joint Committee on Health and Safety.